THE STORY OF
A MUSICAL LIFE

Da Capo Press Music Reprint Series

GENERAL EDITOR

FREDERICK FREEDMAN

VASSAR COLLEGE

THE STORY OF
A MUSICAL LIFE

An Autobiography
by
GEORGE F. ROOT

𝄡 DA CAPO PRESS · NEW YORK · 1970

A Da Capo Press Reprint Edition

This Da Capo Press edition of
The Story of a Musical Life
is an unabridged republication of the
first edition published in Cincinnati in 1891.

Library of Congress Catalog Card Number 70-126072

SBN 306-70031-X
Published by Da Capo Press
A Division of Plenum Publishing Corporation
227 West 17th Street, New York, N.Y. 10011

THE STORY OF
A MUSICAL LIFE

Geo. F. Root

THE STORY

OF

A MUSICAL LIFE.

AN AUTOBIOGRAPHY
BY
GEO. F. ROOT.

CINCINNATI:

PUBLISHED BY THE JOHN CHURCH CO. 74 W. 4TH ST.

———Chicago———   ———New York———
Root & Sons Music Co.   The John Church Co.
200 Wabash Ave.   13 East 16th St.

PREFACE.

OCTOBER 1, 1888, was the fiftieth anniversary of my leaving home to commence my musical life. On that occasion we had a family gathering, at which were commenced the series of narrations which have grown into this book.

They were mostly written in 1889, and that will account for the mention of the names of some people who have died since that time.

Special prominence could have been given in this work to the orderly arrangement of such musical statistics and items of musical history as come within its scope, but such a plan would have interfered with my story, as such, so those matters have been allowed to come in as wanted, without reference to their chronological order.

I do not like the appearance of self-praise that I have to assume while recording in this book certain sayings and events which refer to myself and my career. I hope the reader will see that my story would not be complete without them, and on that ground excuse the apparent egotism. G. F. R.

TABLE OF CONTENTS.

CHAPTER V.

CHAPTER VI.

CHAPTER VII.

CHAPTER VIII.

CHAPTER IX.

CHAPTER XIX.

APPENDIX.

MUSIC.

THE STORY
OF A MUSICAL LIFE.

CHAPTER I.

I WAS born in Sheffield, Mass., August 30, 1820, but my
father moved to North Reading, not far from Boston,
when I was six years old, and there my youth was spent.

I was always very fond of music—not singing at all as a
boy, but playing a little upon every musical instrument that
came in my way. At thirteen I figured that I could " play
a tune " upon as many instruments as I was years old.
Such an achievement in the light of to-day looks entirely
insignificant, but in our isolated village, and in those days, it
was regarded as something rather wonderful. There was a
chronic curiosity in the village choir as to what instrument
the boy would play upon next.

The dream of my life was to be a musician. I did not
know exactly what kind, or how to get started. I thought,
perhaps, I could make a beginning as second flute in some

theater orchestra. It wasn't reputable, I knew (as people regarded the matter then), and relatives and friends were all opposed to it. Indeed, any line of music, as a business, in those days was looked down upon, especially by the more religious and respectable portion of the community. So I knew I should have to fight my way. I ought to except my mother. It was either an unaccountable faith in my ability to succeed, or so much love in her tender heart that she could not bear to thwart me, and she said, " Go, my son, if you find the opportunity; I'll get along in some way." I knew well what that meant—my father and the brother next younger than myself being both in South America, and six younger children to care for—hard times certain—possibly privation; but I had the hardihood of the inexperienced youngster that I was, and said, " Mother, just let me get a start and you shall never want for anything." I thank the Lord that I was able to make that promise good.

But to go on with my story: During the summer of 1838 a member of Mr. A. N. Johnson's choir in Boston spent a few weeks in our village. She had a great deal to say in praise of her teacher as leader and organist, and of his great success as the conductor of the Musical Education Society, to which she also belonged. She described Harmony Hall, on Tremont Row, where the society met and where Mr. Johnson taught, and enlarged generally upon musical matters in that connection until I thought it would be heaven on earth to be in the midst of such opportunities. I did not see how that could ever happen for me, but it did.

Just after the departure of this much-envied member of a Boston choir, a neighbor (a young man a few years older than myself) invited me to go with him to a little town near Worcester, where, as I afterward ascertained, some negotiations of a particular and very interesting nature to him were pending. These, I am happy to say, terminated to his entire satisfaction.

That journey was to me also a very important event. The only railroad going west from Boston then, ended at Worcester. The hardy traveler who would go farther in that direction must climb hills and descend into valleys and wind along by the streams in the old-fashioned stage-coach. It was my first railroad ride, and the luxury of it, and the wonder of it, I shall never forget.

On our return, it was owing to what then seemed a serious dilemma that I was enabled so soon to go to Boston to live. My friend must be at home on the morning of a certain day. To accomplish that, we must be driven from the place of our visit to Worcester to take an afternoon train to Boston, where we were to be met and taken to North Reading at night. Had that program been carried out I should have gone through Boston without stopping, but in Worcester, where we had an hour to wait, my friend went to attend to some matters in which he did not need my company, and I went to the music store, where I became so much absorbed in the instruments and music that when I came to myself the train was gone. There would not be another until the next morning, and I had no money. I was in great trepidation, but soon bethought myself that my mother had a second cousin, who was a theological student, somewhere there. So I trudged out to the seminary, and fortunately found him. He was very kind—"glad to do anything for a son of cousin Sarah"—so he kept me till morning and then gave me money enough to take me home. It is unaccountable that I did not think at the time of that money as anything to be returned. I suppose I associated it with supper, lodging and breakfast as a matter of hospitality, and soon the whole affair passed from my mind. It was perhaps twenty years afterward, on hearing my mother speak of "Cousin Edwin" and his ministry, that I recalled the event, and then came a realizing sense of my delinquency.

It did not take long to figure double compound interest on the amount he gave me, and send him the money.

On my way to Boston I determined to call on Mr. Johnson at Harmony Hall, and see if, by any possibility, there could be an opening for me there. How well I remember ascending the stairs, and knocking at the door. How well I remember the somewhat astonished countenance of the blonde gentleman who let me in. What he said afterward of that interview, not being very complimentary either to my personal appearance or my modesty, I omit, but he did happen to want some one to stay in the room while he was out—to see to the fires and the general order of the place, to answer questions about his engagements, and to make himself generally useful, and he said I might come. He questioned me as to what I could do. Could I sing? No. Could I play at all upon the piano? No. I had seen the keyboard of piano or organ but a few times in my life, but I could play the flute pretty well, and some other instruments a little. Well, the first thing would be to learn to play the piano, and I could practice while he was out, which was most of the time, as the private lessons he then gave were nearly all at the houses of his pupils. I could board at his house, and he would for the present give me three dollars a week beside. This was munificent. Three dollars was a great deal of money. If I could get fitted out with suitable clothes I could save some of my " salary " from the very start, and I knew well what I wanted to do with it.

I have thought many times since how extraordinary it was in Mr. Johnson to take me as he did, for, from his own representation, I could not have been a very promising subject. I do not understand it now, but am glad to think that I could, and did, in some measure, repay his kindness to a friendless boy in the immediate years which followed.

On my way home from Boston, in the old stage-coach,

after the interview and agreement with Mr. Johnson, I was in another world. The ride in the wonderful cars was nothing to this. That was on iron rails, this was in the golden air. The dusty old towns through which we passed were beautiful as never before; even the mulleins by the wayside were transformed into more gorgeous flowers than ever bloomed in garden or conservatory. How often had I felt cramped in the limited surroundings and opportunities of the old home. How many times I have walked, after the day's work was over, through dreary forest roads, to neighboring towns to exercise my musical powers with some embryo performer like myself, or, late "in the stilly night," as a lone serenader, unknown, unexpected and unchallenged, to breathe my sighs for freedom through the old four-keyed flute. But no more of this. I was going where the air was filled with music, and pent-up desires and ambitions could have unlimited freedom.

There was great excitement when I reached home. I was really going to Boston to study music—must be at my post on the first day of the next month. On the strength of my prospects I borrowed a little money of my grandmother for an outfit, and went around telling the good news to interested and sympathizing neighbors. All met me with good words. "Go ahead!" they said; "we'll lend a hand on the farm if we're needed." They believed in me musically, and as for my mother there was not a person in the town who would not do her a kindness if he had the opportunity.

At last the important first day of October arrived. I wheeled my trunk down the willow lane to the main road, about a quarter of a mile (our place was called "Willow Farm"), to wait for the old stage-coach that lumbered by every morning on its way to the city. An hour passed and no stage. I forget how I found out that it had been taken off—had made its last journey the day before. The new railroad from Lowell to Boston had taken so many of its passengers that it would no longer pay to run it. But I must get to Boston that day. What was I to do? Our nearest neighbor, " Uncle Mike," as everybody called him said: " Why, we'll make that very railroad carry ye there. Old Pete and I'll take ye over to Wilmin'ton, and you'll catch the cars afore night." So Uncle Mike harnessed up and took trunk and me six miles to the new railroad, where, by good fortune, I had not long to wait for a train. Then, with thanks and a good-bye to the old neighbor, I left for aye the old life, and in due time arrived in the city, and at Mr. Johnson's house at the "North End."

The next morning I commenced the duties and pleasures of my new vocation in Harmony Hall, as Mr. Johnson's music-room was called. This place was leased by the Musical Education Society, but Mr. Johnson had the use of it for conducting the society once a week. It was a light, cheerful room, up one flight of stairs; a platform, with a piano on it at one end, and a little curtained office, with a desk, at the other. After being told what my duties in regard to fires and care of room would be, I went with eagerness to the piano for my first lesson. The idea of calling it drudgery—this making musical sounds upon a pianoforte—nothing could be more absurd, as it seemed to me. It was a delight, even though my large, clumsy fingers would go right in the simplest exercises of Hunten's Instruction book only by the most laborious practice. But that was cheerfully given. Every minute when Mr. Johnson was out, or when I was not answering a call at the door, I was at work, and during Mr. Johnson's lessons in the room, while I was out of sight at the curtained desk, I was trying to get some flexibility into my stubborn fingers, while looking over some music-book. I had learned to read the notes of simple music both on treble and base staffs by the various instruments I had played.

When I say I had never sung, I do not mean that I had never used my voice at all in that way. I had occasionally joined in the base of simple church tunes, but was never encouraged by listeners to continue my performances long, or to make them prominent. It was always:—"George, you'd better take your flute." But Mr. Johnson said that if I was going to teach I ought to be able to use my voice correctly, and sing at least enough to give examples of tone and pitch. I dare say he saw then, what I realized after awhile, that I had begun too late to make much of a player upon piano or organ, and that if I developed any gift for teaching, my success must be in singing-classes and other vocal work. So I went at it. I sang in the Musical Education Society and in Mr. Johnson's choir at the Odeon, and often growled a base to my five-finger exercises while practicing.

But here I ought to say something about the condition of music in our part of the country in those days. Not many years before, a singing-school had been held in the old red school-house, where "faw, sol, law, faw, sol, law, me, faw," were the syllables for the scale—where one must find the "*me* note" (seven) to ascertain what key he was singing in, and where some of the old "fuguing tunes," as they were called, were still sung. I well remember how, shortly after, we heard that a new system of teaching music had been introduced into Boston, in which they used a blackboard and sang "do, re, mi," etc., to the scale. But how silly "do" sounded. We thought it smart to say that the man who invented that was a *dough*-head, and how flat were *fa* and *la*, in comparison with the dignified "faw" and "law." Later, however, when some tunes connected with the new movement came, we changed our minds about the man who was at the head of it. Nothing before, so heavenly, had been heard as the melody to "Thus far the Lord hath led me on" (Hebron); and one of the great things in going to Boston was that I should probably see LOWELL MASON.

It is an interesting fact that some music, at every grade, from lowest to highest, has in it that mysterious quality which makes it live, while all the rest fades away and is forgotten. Sometimes I think the more we know the less keen are our perceptions in regard to that divine afflatus. We understand better the construction of the music we hear, but do not feel, as in more unsophisticated states, the thrill of that mysterious life—at least I do not, and I put it forth as a possibly true theory in general, because every tune that produced that enchanting effect upon me then, lives in the hearts of the people now, while those that did not have dropped out of use.

Certain it is, if music writers and publishers could know of every composition whether it had in it that mysterious vitality or not, there would be far less music issued, for but few musical compositions in proportion to the number printed have in them the elements even of a short life.

I worked steadily at my piano lessons, and got on well, considering the obstacles I had to overcome in my grown-up hands. But piano playing was not then what it is now, by a difference that it would be hard to describe. A piano in a country town was a rarity, and a person even in Boston who could play as well as hundreds of young people all over the country now play, would have attracted universal attention.

I think I could not have been practicing more than two weeks before Mr. Johnson started me in the playing of chords by the method that has since been so well known under the name of Johnson's Thorough Base. By this means I was to learn to play Hebron and Ward and Ham-

burg and Boylston, and all those tunes that had moved me
as no music had ever done before. I need not say that I
worked with a will, but I remember well that I was in a
chronic state of astonishment that my hands would *not* do
what I saw so clearly should be done, and that I must play
a succession of chords over so many, many times before
they would go without a hitch.

It was not long after this that Mr. Johnson said to me
one day; "I wish you would learn two of those tunes to
play at the Wednesday night prayer-meeting." "What! play
for the people to sing?" "Yes; you can do it; you need not
play the tune through first; just play the first chord, and
then start, and they'll all go with you. It will be all the
more sure if you sing the first word or two." "But I shall
make some mistakes, I'm afraid." "Well, if you do they
won't be noticed." "But I may run against a stump and
stop." "Well, they'll go on, and you can catch up at your
leisure." Talk about courage! I mean on Mr. Johnson's part.
He would take more and greater risks of that sort than any
man I ever knew. But he knew I would strain every nerve
to accomplish what he wished, and he always said he could
rely on my—I think "self-confidence" was the term he used,
but there is a much shorter word now coming into our vocabulary which would perhaps have expressed his meaning
more forcibly. However, I went through it, and after that,
for some months, prepared my two tunes every week for the
prayer-meeting.

This church arrangement was peculiar. It was a Congregational church, under the pastoral care of Rev. Wm. M.
Rogers, then one of the most popular clergymen of Boston.
Its services were held in what had been the Federal St. Theater (corner of Federal and Franklin Streets), but was now
called the "Odeon." It was owned or leased by a new organization called the "Boston Academy of Music," and used

exclusively by that association and this Congregational church. It had been somewhat remodeled, though it had still the theater look. The stage was fitted with raised seats for a large chorus. There was a large organ at the back, and a conductor's platform in front, occupied on Sundays by the minister's pulpit. Lowell Mason was at the head of the Boston Academy of Music, and the conductor of its large chorus, and George James Webb was the organist, but on Sundays Mr. Johnson was the organist, and his choir the performers. The prayer-meetings were held in a long room over the front entrance, called " The Saloon." I don't think that word was then used at all as the name of a drinking place. It had more the signification of drawing-room or parlor. I don't know how it came to be applied to that little hall, but as I remember the notices, they would sound strangely now :—"The Sunday-school after service in the *saloon;*" "The ladies' meeting Tuesday afternoon in the *saloon;*" "The prayer-meeting Wednesday evening in the *saloon;*" and there we had our choir rehearsals, and later, singing classes, so that in those days that word became connected in my mind with all that was "pure and lovely and of good report," instead of bearing the bad signification which attaches to it now.

CHAPTER II.

1838–1839, BOSTON—MY FIRST PUPIL—A NEW BARGAIN—THE
FLUTE CLUB—FIRST VOICE LESSONS—SOME OF THE PROM-
INENT TEACHERS, AUTHORS, AND CONCERT PERFORMERS
OF EARLY DAYS—DAVID AND GOLIATH—SOME REMARKS
ABOUT SIMPLE MUSIC—MY FIRST SINGING CLASS—MR.
WOODBURY—MY VENERABLE PUPIL FROM MAINE—THE
"OLD CORNER BOOKSTORE."

I DO not think it could have been more than six weeks
from my beginning with Mr. Johnson that I had another surprise. One day a young man called to inquire
about taking lessons upon the piano. He was a mechanic
—an apprentice to a jeweler I think. Mr. Johnson asked
him if he could play at all. No, he knew nothing about
music whatever. Mr. Johnson reflected a moment and then
said, as if it were the result of very serious and important
deliberation: "I think my assistant here, Mr. Root, would
be best adapted to your case." My astonishment was unbounded, but if this young man knew nothing I was a little
ahead of him, and it would be a delight to help him over the
road I had just traveled. That was my first pupil, and what
I lacked in experience I made up in good will and attention.
At any rate he was well satisfied, as I had good reason to
know afterward. It was not long before others came and
inquired for me instead of Mr. Johnson, on account of young
Slade's recommendation.

About this time, certainly not more than seven weeks
from the beginning of my connection with Mr. Johnson, he
proposed a new bargain. The first had not been for any

definite time—we were "to see how we liked," as he said, but of course the seeing was wholly on his side. He had now evidently made up his mind, and an agreement was made for a year at a very considerable increase in pay. That I was glad and thankful goes without saying. The news flew to the old farm as fast as Uncle Sam's machinery in those days could take it (there was no dream yet for years of telegraph), and at "Thanksgiving," toward the end of November, when I made my first visit home, we had a happy time, as you may imagine.

About this time Mr. Mason advertised that new members would be admitted to the Boston Academy's Chorus. Those who wished to join must be at a certain place at a certain time, and have their voices and reading ability tested. Mr. Johnson said I had better go; that the Academy's work was more difficult than that of the Musical Education Society, and that the practice would be good for me in every way. I shook in my shoes at the suggestion, but Mr. Johnson's courage was equal to the occasion, and I went. That was my first sight of Lowell Mason, and also of Geo. Jas. Webb, who did the trying of the voices, while Mr. Mason looked on. I passed, and was much surprised when Mr. Mason came to where I was sitting and asked me to join his choir—that famous Bowdoin Street Choir, the like of which has rarely been equaled, in my opinion, in this or any other country. I told him why I could not—that I was with Mr. Johnson, etc., but that invitation settled the voice question in my mind. I was going to sing. Lowell Mason had wanted me in his choir, and that was as good as a warranty that I could succeed.

Meanwhile I did not neglect my flute. I was so well along on that that Mr. Johnson thought something might come of it. So I took some lessons and gave some lessons on that instrument, and some time in the following year I organized a flute club of my pupils and others. There were some pretty good singers in it, and we called it the "Nicholson Flute and Glee Club." "Nicholson's Flute Instructor" was my delight, both for method and music, hence the name. We had music arranged in six parts for our ten flutes. Simon Knaebel, a good orchestra and band musician, I remember, did the arranging. We had marches, quicksteps, waltzes, etc., all simple but popular then. We gave some concerts in the neighboring towns, and on one grand occasion played at some performance in the Odeon, and, what is better, were encored. It was rather absurd to have harmony, the base of which could go no lower than middle C; but it was a novelty, and to us a source of great enjoyment.

One important day, soon after my admission to the Boston Academy's Chorus, Mr. Johnson said I had better take some voice lessons of Mr. Webb; that private voice teaching was very profitable, and he thought I could fit myself to do that work. Mr. Johnson never flinched from what he thought I ought to do. I was glad enough, however, to take lessons of Geo. Jas. Webb, the best vocal teacher in Boston, an elegant organist, an accomplished musician, and a model Christian gentleman. He received me with great kindness, and after trying my voice in various ways, gave me some exercises to work upon. At my next lesson, after I had sung what he had before given me to practice, he looked up with an expression of pleased surprise and said: "Well, Mr. Root, I believe you *will* learn to sing." I replied, "Of course; that is what I fully intend to do." "Ah, but," he responded, "at your first lesson I thought it extremely doubtful whether it would be worth your while to try." Of course he had reference to solo singing, and not to joining with the bases in a chorus, which I could then do fairly well.

My lessons went on with him for months—a year, perhaps, and I came not only to delight in them, but in the friendly atmosphere of his pleasant home.   I used always to be glad when I could see his little Mary—four or five years old perhaps; she was so bright and so full of music.   Once I remember she came into the teaching room, where I was waiting for my lesson, and said: " Papa will come pretty soon, but I've been to the 'Rainers.' " The Rainers were a family of Swiss Yodlers, the first, I think, to come to this country, and were singing in costume and in their native language their pretty Swiss songs.   Everybody went to hear them.   "I've been to the Rainers," she went on, as she climbed upon the piano stool, "and wasn't it funny what they said?"   Here she piped up with a comical motion of her head, but with accordant tones on the piano :—

Take a   piece a   yarn, Take a   piece a   yarn.

Mr. Webb, coming in at that moment, laughed and explained that Mary was very fond of giving her imitation of Simon Rainer's manner and her translation of his German.   I thought often of this little incident in after years, while listening to her splendid rendering of " I know that my Redeemer liveth," or some other oratorio classic, and later, while enjoying her gracious hospitality as the wife of Dr. William Mason, in their lovely home in Orange, New Jersey.

Speaking of foreign performers, it was about this time that we heard Herwig, who was, I think, the first really great violinist to come to this country.   His harmonic playing—making his violin sound like a fine high wind instrument, caused great astonishment, and filled his houses to overflowing.   It was some years afterward that we heard Vieuxtemps, Sivori, and Ole Bull on his first visit, but Artot came soon after Herwig.   About that time also came the

first pianists that much excelled the best we had heard. Jane
Sloman was first, and in a few months Rakemann. They
had great success then, but such playing now would be considered only mediocre—I mean as concert playing. Every
large city in the country has better players.

But a matter of greater interest to me was the advent in
those days of Braham, who had been for a generation the
greatest English tenor. He was an old man, and it was said
his voice was not what it had been, but no one who then
heard him sing "Thou shalt dash them in pieces like a pot-
ter's vessel " probably ever heard anything before or since
to compare with his tone upon the word "dash"—so large
and at the same time so terrifically intense. Marcus Colburn, one of our resident tenors, came the nearest to him in
power, and would have made as great a singer probably,
if he had had the opportunity, for his voice excelled Braham's in a certain sweet and ringing quality.

That brings to my mind a rather ludicrous scene in
which Mr. Colburn and I were chief actors. Mr. Colburn
was a giant in size, over six feet in height, and very portly
—weighing probably near to three hundred pounds. After I
came to be regarded as a promising base singer it came about
—I don't remember whether through Mr. Johnson's courage
or that of some one else — that I was appointed to sing
with Mr. Colburn from Neukomm's Oratorio of " David " the
duet between David and Goliath, at a concert at the Odeon.
It was absurd enough when we went forward together to
begin, for this giant was David, and I, a stripling in comparison to him, was Goliath ; but when I had to sing, in the
most ponderous tones I could assume, "I can not war with
boys," the audience broke out into irrepressible laughter, in
which Colburn, who had the most contagious laugh in the
world, joined, and that " broke me all up," as they say now-
a-days. We went through our performance, however, though
we did not consider it an unqualified success.

But the most important event to me, in the way of public performances, in those days (1839), was the singing of Henry Russell, an English Jew, who composed and sang "The Ivy Green," "Our Native Song," "A Life on the Ocean Wave," "The Old Sexton," "Wind of the Winter Night," and many other songs of that grade. He had a beautiful baritone voice and great command of the keyboard—played his own accompaniments, gave his concerts entirely alone, and in a year in this country made a fortune. Songs of his, like "The Maniac" and "The Gambler's Wife," were exceedingly pathetic, and always made people cry when he sang them. He looked so pitiful and so sympathetic— "he felt every word," as his listeners would think and say —and yet, when he retired to his dressing room, he was said to have been much amused at the grief of his weeping constituents, showing that he had not really the heart in his song that he appeared to have.

Of course it is a part of the singer's art to assume emotions that he does not really feel, and that is all right if the emotions he assumes are healthful and good. For instance, a man may sing of the delights of a farmer's or a sailor's life in such a way as to make his hearers think he likes that life best, when, in point of fact, he may much prefer some other. But good taste requires that the singer should treat respectfully the emotion he excites.

I was so taken with Russell's songs that I worked harder than ever before to be able to play and sing them as he did. When the accompaniments were too much for me, or the pitch too high, I modified and simplified and transposed, and in a few months had them at my tongue's and fingers' ends, and I have sung certain of them ever since — more than fifty years. While Russell was in this country, Joseph Philip Knight came over and gave us "Rocked in the Cradle of the Deep," which Russell added to his repertoire, and I, with certain modifications, to mine.

This is a good place to speak of the absurdity of saying that simple music keeps the tastes and musical culture of the people down. You might as well say that a person is kept in addition, subtraction, multiplication and division by having around him more examples in elementary arithmetic than he needs. If he is interested in the subject, he'll go on after he has mastered the simpler to that which is more difficult, if the examples or books that he needs are within his reach. You can not keep him in the lower grade by multiplying elementary books. If he is not interested, or is more occupied with other things, he may never go beyond those elementary mathematics which are needed for the common duties of life; but since he can not get higher *without going through them*, it is useless to put that which is higher before him *until they are mastered.*

For a few months Russell's songs filled me with delight. They were just what I needed to help me out of my elementary condition. Before a year was over they had done their work, and I craved something higher. Schubert's songs came next. Is it supposed for an instant that songs of the Russell grade, had they been multiplied a hundred-fold, would have had any effect in keeping me back, if I could get what I wanted? Certainly not; and Schubert's songs, and others of that grade, were, and are, plenty, and more easily obtained, because, being non-copyright, they are free to all publishers. Those not in music, or not so musical naturally, do not get through the elementary state so soon; in fact, many business and professional people, giving very little time or thought to the subject, never get through; they prefer the simpler music to the end of their days. But there is no royal road for such. They must get their fill of the simple—must hear it until they crave something higher —before that which is higher can be of any use to them. It is an axiom that emotional or æsthetic benefit by music

can come to a person only through music that he likes.   By
that alone can he grow musically.

Just as the elementary departments of mathematics are
the foundations of that great subject, so tonic, dominant and
sub-dominant (the simplest harmonies) are foundations in
all music—the highest as well as the lowest.   No one de-
rides or looks with contempt upon the elements of mathematics, or upon the thousand ways by which those simpler
things are made interesting to the learner.   On the contrary, the most learned mathematicians appreciate their importance and delight in their success.   So it should be in
our science and art; and, without apologizing for what is in-
correct or untasteful in the simple music of the day, I say,
unhesitatingly, that all correct musical forms, however elementary, find some one to whom they are just what is
needed, either for practical or æsthetic benefit, or both.
Since, therefore, there are always so many grown-up men
and women, learned and strong in other things, who are
still in elementary musical states, I keep, ready for use, the
simple songs that helped me, and am always glad to sing
them where they will do any good.

I do not quite remember where my first "singing-
school" was taught, but I think an experimental class was
held in Harmony Hall during my first winter (1838–9), under the guise of helping some young ladies and gentlemen
to "read notes," who were desirous of joining the Musical
Education Society.   I had seen Mr. Johnson teach a few
times, but I had no orderly method, and my work must have
been exceedingly desultory and crude.   Something carried
me through, however, and the next autumn I had a large
class at the North End, which lasted nearly through the
winter, and which, on the closing night, made me very
proud and happy by the gift of a silver goblet, suitably en-
graved, and which now occupies a place among my treas-
ures.

About this time I became acquainted with I. B. Woodbury. He was two or three years older than myself, and had commenced his musical work a year or two before me. He had a small room, also, in Tremont Row. He was a most indefatigable student and worker. I think it was during my first winter in Boston that he taught a singing-school in Beverly, and often walked back to Boston, fifteen miles, after nine o'clock at night, to be ready for his lessons in the morning. We who were inured to the hardships of New England country life in those days did not think of such things as they would be thought of now. Mr. Woodbury was very economical, and in a year or two had saved enough money to go to London and take lessons for a few months. Soon after he came home he began to write, and it was not long before he published his first book of church music. He was prosperous and very ambitious. He said to me once, "When I die I shall surprise the world," and he did. He was not strong constitutionally, and the flame burned so fiercely that the end for him came early. It was then found that he had left almost his entire estate to found a Musical Institution—the money to be used for that purpose after it had been invested long enough to produce a certain sum. But the law stepped in and changed this disposition of his fortune in favor of his wife and children. Mr. Woodbury was a genial, pleasant gentleman, and because he wrote only simple music, never was credited (by those who did not know him) with the musical ability and culture that he really possessed.

Speaking of Mr. Woodbury's long walk, and the hardihood of New England country boys, reminds me of what I used sometimes to do to be home on Thanksgiving Day. That was then by far the greatest day of the year in New England, viewed in a social or religious way. Christmas was hardly noticed. Everybody would be at the father's or grandfather's home for "Thanksgiving," if within the bounds of possibility. If I had a singing-school the night before, I would start, after a short sleep, perhaps at two or three o'clock in the morning, and walk homeward, somebody starting from there at the same time in a wagon to meet me, so that I might be at home for breakfast. Once, after my father returned from South America, a young man from North Reading, who was learning a trade in Boston, took this walk with me. We were in the highest state of boyish exhilaration, and when my companion suggested that it would be a good scheme to be on the lookout for the wagon, and, when we heard it, to conceal ourselves and surprise horse and rider in highwayman fashion, I agreed. It was my father whom we met, and it was a lonely part of the road. We sprang out at the horse, and he said : " Hullo! what are ye about? " and immediately added when he saw who we were : " Boys, this would have been anything but a Thanksgiving Day for us if I had been armed as I was in South America." We saw at once how foolish we had been, although, as no one carried arms in those days, no idea of risk came to our minds. We did not tell of our exploit at home, but I have often thought how my father " stood fire," and what crestfallen highwaymen we were for the rest of the journey.

I must not omit to speak of one most interesting pupil that I had during my second year in Harmony Hall. One day I answered a gentle rap at the door, and a large, fine-looking old gentleman entered. He said : " I suppose you will think it strange that an old man like me should wish to learn to play upon the organ, but I have a small one in my house (there were no reed organs then), and if I could learn to play a few of my favorite tunes upon it I should be very glad. I live in Farmington, Maine, but am spending a few days with my son in the city here." I told him that he could not do much in a few days, but that I would do my best for him if he decided to try. He did so decide, and seemed to enjoy the lessons, as I certainly did his acquaintance, although he did not accomplish all he had hoped in the way of learning his favorite tunes. He was a typical New Englander, of the best kind of those days—one who had lived a long, blameless life, practicing all the virtues of the Puritans without their hardness. His quaint, shrewd remarks were a constant source of pleasure and benefit, for they were from the "innocence of wisdom."

I mention this circumstance, first, because this lovely old gentleman was the father of the brothers Abbott, the oldest of whom was Jacob Abbott, the author of "The Young Christian" and "The Corner Stone," and later of the "Rollo" books, and grandfather of Dr. Lyman Abbott, the present pastor of Plymouth Church, Brooklyn, and editor of the *Christian Union*, and of Benjamin V. and Austin Abbott, distinguished lawyers and legal authors in New York City. I also mention this circumstance because it led to an important change in my life and prospects four years later.

I must not omit to speak of the "Old Corner Bookstore," which still stands at the corner of School and Washington Streets. It was a bookstore then as now, only at that time, on one side, with one counter, was the sheet-music and music-book establishment of "Parker & Ditson." I went there often for music, and was often waited upon by the handsome, dark-eyed junior partner of the concern—the man who then was making the beginning of what is now one of the largest music houses in the world.

CHAPTER III.

1840–1844, BOSTON—PARTNERSHIP—FIRST EFFORTS AS ORGAN-
IST AND CHOIR LEADER—THE FIRST TEACHING OF MUSIC
IN PUBLIC SCHOOLS—THE TEACHERS' CLASS OF THE BOS-
TON ACADEMY OF MUSIC AND MY FIRST EFFORTS AT
VOCAL TRAINING IN CLASSES—THE OLD MARLBORO' AND
MY UNINTENTIONAL CRITIC—BOWDOIN ST. CHOIR AND MY
INTENTIONAL CRITIC—BOSTON'S FIRST BOAT CLUB—CALL
TO NEW YORK.

A GREAT change for me, in fact for both of us, took
place before my first year's agreement with Mr. Johnson was out. He proposed a partnership for five years, in
which he should have two-thirds and I one-third of what we
both should earn, he to have the privilege of spending one
of the years in Germany, the division of profits to be the
same during his absence. I agreed, and the plan was carried
out, and now I can not be quite sure of the dates of certain
things, for the Chicago fire destroyed my records of those
days, and of many years after. But I shall be near enough
for the purposes of this story.

It was not long after our partnership agreement (probably about 1840) that Mr. Johnson was called to take charge
of the choir and play the organ in Park Street Church—
the first church then in point of size and importance in
the Congregational denomination of the city. I had long
before commenced my organ performances by playing the
" last tune " at the Odeon services, in which all the people
joined, and which was always well known and simple, and
then, as soon as Mr. Johnson's courage was equal to it, I

supplied an organist's place for six months at Mr. Budding-
ton's church in Charlestown, just across the bridge. This
was my first organ engagement. Mr. Johnson still had the
choir at Mr. Rogers' church, and now was to play half a day
at each place, I playing the other half. Whether the Odeon
church (the Central Congregational) had yet moved to its
new edifice in Winter street, built near the spot where the
Music Hall now stands, I am not certain; but if not yet, it
was accomplished soon after. Then all went smoothly in
regard to the two choirs—they were near neighbors and
often met together for general practice. There were about
thirty voices in each choir.

Mr. Johnson had had a rigid business training in a large
hardware store in Boston before he made music his entire
occupation, and always had the idea of making ours a business establishment, modeled strictly on business principles.
I was his first "apprentice;" I became afterward "confiden-
tial clerk," and later, partner, and he would now have others
coming along in the same way. So, soon after the arrangement with the Park Street Church, he decided to give up
Harmony Hall and take three rooms in the fine basement
of that church facing the Common. I remonstrated gently,
for the new rooms would cost us $600 a year, and $600 then
was as much for most purposes as twice that sum would be
now. But he said we could there have a fine sign out; that
we could raise our prices, take a new student or two, and
increase the business generally, enough to more than pay
the extra expense. We certainly did have our hands full,
but we probably should have had that at the old place.
Nothing, however, could be more convenient for our purposes than those rooms, and the outlook under the great
trees of the Common was most picturesque and beautiful.

About the time I went to Boston, Lowell Mason told the
public school authorities of the city that he believed vocal

music could be successfully taught in the schools as a regular branch of education, and that if they would allow him he would teach in one or two for a year without pay, to show that it could be done.   Music in public schools was then an unheard-of thing in this country, but Mr. Mason's experiment was tried, and it resulted in the introduction of music into the entire school system of the city, with Mr. Mason for musical superintendent.   The first year Mr. Mason and Mr. J. C. Woodman (of whom I will speak more at length later) taught in all the schools.   The second year Mr. Mason employed Mr. Johnson and myself to help, and taught less himself.   I taught in five of the schools, and I think Mr. Johnson had the same number.   A course was marked out which took a year, each school receiving two half-hour lessons a week.

One of my schools was on Fort Hill, an elevation, as I remember it, of eighty or a hundred feet above the surrounding houses.   I had no occasion to go into that part of the city for many years after I left it, and not very long ago, when I thought I would climb the old hill again, not a vestige of it remained.   It was as flat all about there as Chicago. But when I meet Mr. Haines, the partner and now practical head of the great Ditson establishment, it is the same face that used always to give me a friendly greeting from behind his desk at the Mason street school, when I appeared there for the singing lesson; so of a distinguished banker in Cincinnati whom I occasionally see; and a successful Chicago merchant who is a near neighbor—all were boys in the Mason street school.

If my getting on so fast in a city like Boston seems unaccountable, I must explain again that music was in a very different condition then from what it is now.   It was just emerging from the florid but crude melodies and the imperfect harmonies of the older time.   Lowell Mason had but just commenced what proved to be a revolution in the "plain song" of the church and of the people, and his methods of teaching the elementary principles of music were so much better and so much more attractive than anything that had before been seen that those who were early in the field had very great advantage. We had no competition and were sought for on every hand. To be sure there were organists then who would be considered fine organists now, but such very moderate players as we were, got on, because our choirs produced the new kind of simple, sweet music that went to the hearts of the people and the people connected the organ, little as there was in the playing, with the general effect they so much enjoyed. It was very much like the success of an early dealer in pianos in Chicago, who used to sell a great number of instruments by sitting down to them and singing a song while playing two or three simple chords. It must be a fine piano to be connected with such soul-stirring music.

One of the things that spurred me up from the first to do my best to succeed was the consciousness that if my father should return from South America and find my experiment a failure—having left mother and the children as I did, that I should not feel entirely comfortable in the paternal society, for his own effort to better the family fortunes had not been very successful. But during my second year with Mr. Johnson he returned and no fault was found. On the contrary, he went back to the old farm and enjoyed my prosperity with the rest of us. My brother (E. T. Root, who, years afterward, with C. M. Cady, started the firm of Root & Cady in Chicago) came home from South America, where he had gone for his health, a few months before my father, and soon found a situation in Boston where he could devote a part of his time to music. It was not long, however, before he decided to make music his business, as I had done. So we sent a piano up to the old red house, and he went home and gave himself wholly to practice. He was always the singer of the family. Before his voice changed it was a beautiful soprano, and after the change a smooth, sympathetic tenor; but more of that later. My sisters, too, practiced whenever they could get at the piano, and all played and sang, much to their enjoyment and advantage in following years. Indeed, my youngest sister, who was a baby when I left home, has been for some years one of the best and most successful voice teachers in the profession, as all the musical people of Chicago will testify.

It was perhaps the year before I went to Boston that Lowell Mason and Geo. Jas. Webb held the first "Musical Convention," but they did not call the gathering by that name. It was for some years "The Teachers' Class of the Boston Academy of Music." Its sessions continued for ten days, and brought together teachers of music and choir leaders from city and country. These being mostly men, the Academy's chorus, Mr. Mason's choir and other singers of the city joined for the afternoon and evening practice and performances. The mornings were spent by Mr. Mason in showing his new method of teaching and in giving his ideas of church music; the afternoons with Mr. Webb in part-song, glee and madrigal singing, and in the evening, when all could come, the choruses of the great masters were sung, Mr. Mason conducting and Mr. Webb accompanying upon the organ. Mr. Mason was a strong conductor and an intelligent interpreter of those great works, and Mr. Webb, the most refined and delightful teacher of the English glee and madrigal that I have ever known.

It was at the Teachers' Class of 1841, I think, that I began to figure as an instructor in that kind of work. It came about in this way: — I noticed that the voices, especially the bases, were, many of them, pinched and hard, and I thought I would see if I could help them. There had been no voice training in classes then; that work had been done entirely by private instruction. So, in pursuance of my plan, I told some of the men of the class privately to meet me during the noon recess in the saloon (the small hall of the Odeon of which I have spoken) and we would see if our voices were all right. Singers, especially those in elementary states, are always interested in that subject, so the proposition met with a hearty response. There were perhaps twenty present at that first meeting. I took each one separately, all the rest looking on or occasionally joining, and sang a tone with him either an octave higher or an octave lower, and showed him and all how much more resonance and blending there was when the tone was produced with the throat more open, and when he could not readily change from the way to which he had been accustomed, I devised such means as I could think of to help him, much to the interest of the class and sometimes to their great amusement. When I got through there was a good deal of favorable excitement in the little company. "This is what we want. Can't we have this every day?" was heard on all sides. I said I was willing enough, but they would have to go to Mr. Mason about it; we certainly could not meet at this time every day, for some of us had then lost our dinners.

When the class came together for Mr. Webb's exercise in the afternoon, these men gathered about Mr. Mason and told him what they wanted. They were so close to him, and so clamorous I remember, that he jumped up into a chair, and when he fully understood the situation, announced that the last hour of the morning would be devoted to vocal training under the instruction of Mr. Root. This was my first appearance in vocal training class-work. Of course I could not hear voices alone so much after this as I had done in the smaller and more informal gathering, but it was better than nothing, and as there was no previous work of the kind to compare it with, it was popular, and continued as one of the features of teachers' classes and conventions during my long connection with Mr. Mason, and has been an integral part of normals and conventions ever since.

It may be worth mentioning that in the Spring of my third year in Boston the first Boat Club of that city was formed. It consisted of twenty-four young men (two crews), mostly members of Park Street and Winter Street Churches. We had a boat house on Beacon street, where now are magnificent residences, and used often to row up near to the Common where the Public Garden now is. All was open water where Commonwealth avenue and those finest buildings of Boston now are; the only obstructions were the railroads on piles and bridges that ran across the back bay. There was then, as to-day, the "mill dam," and the long bridge to Cambridge, and the bridges to Charlestown, to pass, when we wanted to row down the harbor. Ours was a ten-oared boat that had belonged to the Yale College Club at New Haven. We named it the "Shawmut" (the old Indian name for Boston), and our club was called the "Shawmut Boat Club." There was room enough in the boat for six guests, and in her we had many pleasant excursions up the rivers and down among the islands of the harbor, and much delight and advantage from the open air and the rowing. I take pleasure in recalling that I was the first president of the club.

After everything was well under way at the Park Street and Winter Street Churches (about 1841), and all my time was occupied in teaching, Mr. Johnson went to Germany. During his absence I taught both choirs, and Mr. S. A. Bancroft, who had taken some lessons from us, and who afterward became one of the prominent organists of Boston, played the "other half-day." I now took up my quarters at the Marlboro' Hotel, on Washington street, opposite the head of Franklin street. This was a temperance and religious house, our excellent landlord, Mr. Nathaniel Rogers, conducting family prayers in the public parlor every morning. Church and temperance people from all over the country gathered there, and I made many valuable acquaintances from among them during the two years that I was one of the family. One friend was made in a rather curious way. I was standing at one of the parlor windows, looking down Franklin street one Sunday afternoon after service, observing the people pouring up from the principal Catholic church, which was then on Franklin near Federal street, and talking with some of my young fellow-boarders, when a gentleman joined us and asked where all the people were coming from. I answered him, and then he asked about other churches of the city, and, finding I could tell him what he wanted to know, he began to ask about the music of the different denominations and then about the organists of the city. Presently he said, "I was at Park Street Church this afternoon, and I found it there as almost everywhere—the organist seemed to think the organ was everything. He played so loud that the voices of the choir were almost drowned." Here my companions, who stood about, became suddenly interested and glanced mischievously at each other and at me. I replied that in the summer it was often the case in chorus choirs that the leading voices were away and the organist had to play louder than he liked, to bolster up the others. He did not seem to think that was a very good excuse, and soon came the question I dreaded: "Do you know who the organist is at Park Street Church?" If my mischievous companions had not been there I should have spared him and myself in some way, but as it was I could not flinch, and answered that I was the individual. He was a good deal embarrassed, but I helped him out by saying that the reasons

I had given were the real ones in my case, and that if he would come and hear us at our best he would not have to find that fault with the accompaniment. It turned out that he was a lawyer from Troy, very fond of music and something of an organist. He seemed to appreciate my efforts to relieve his embarrassment, and the interview terminated in a very pleasant way. The next day we went to see some of the fine organs of the city, and two or three years afterward, when Messrs. Mason and Webb held a musical convention in Troy, in which I did my usual voice work, this gentleman was an interested and helpful friend to us throughout the session. But this incident taught me a lesson in regard to saying unpleasant things about a person unless I know to whom I am talking.

In due time Mr. Johnson returned. He had studied harmony a year or more under Schneider von Wartensee, at Frankfort, and once when he went for his lesson had heard Mendelssohn play one of his new compositions to the old harmonist. I was much impressed with Mr. Johnson's description of the way the old man said "schön" at the close of the performance, and of Mendelssohn's pleasure at the approval of the man who almost never spoke a word of praise. I do not remember anything very eventful in our affairs for a while after Mr. Johnson's return.

Mr. Mason used occasionally to call at our rooms, sometimes leading a small boy who was then practicing his first lessons upon the piano. That boy was his son William, the now well-known and distinguished pianist and composer, and the strong and true friend of musical education in this country.

Mr. Jacob Abbott used to stop at the " Marlboro " when he came into the city, and I remember once taking him out for a boat ride in the "Shawmut." He was greatly interested in the working of the boat, and especially in the nautical terms employed in directing the ten oarsmen and the bow-man. We went through all the maneuvers we knew for his especial benefit. All of these appear in " Uncle George's " directions to Rollo and the boys on the formation of their boat club, in one of the " Rollo Books " published not long after.

Something less than a year remained of my engagement with Mr. Johnson when a change took place in our church matters. For some reason Mr. Mason decided that he would rather be at Winter Street (Central) Church, and what he wished was generally accomplished in those days, so it was arranged that he should come there where Mr. Johnson and I had had charge, and that I should go to Bowdoin street, Mr. Johnson remaining at Park street. It was hard for me to follow Mr. Mason and his magnificent choir with any hope of success, but all the people who were interested realized my difficulty and were very consid-erate and kind. If there were complaints or unpleasant comparisons they never came to my ears. It was thought best that my headquarters should be Bowdoin street, the convenient rooms that Mr. Mason had used for teaching being placed at my disposal, so I made an amicable arrange-ment with Mr. Johnson for the balance of my five years' agreement and commenced on my own account. Most of Mr. Mason's choir went with him. Of those who remained my memory dwells most upon one of whom I have often thought since that he denied himself the advantages and enjoyment of his place in the best choir in the country to help me in my difficult undertaking, but his way was so peculiar (so good in some respects) that I mention it here. He was one of Mr. Mason's best base singers, both in the Academy's chorus and in the choir, considerably older than myself, a prosperous business man, prominent in the church and in the Sunday-school, opinionated, decided and out-

spoken on every question in which he took an interest, but
with clear-cut ideas of subordination which had been inten-
sified by his long course of training under the best musical
disciplinarian that this country has ever seen. I did not
know all this then, although I had been acquainted with
him for two or three years, so was in some anxiety when I
learned that he was going to stay at Bowdoin street, lest I
might find it difficult to be master of the situation. It was
with considerable trepidation that I went to the first rehearsal, but instead of greeting me in his outspoken way or
patronizing me as I feared he would, my friend was seated
in his place, not saying a word to any one. It was time to
begin, but I had been delayed by one thing and another and
was a little behind time in starting. I knew how exact
everything had been there, and thought that perhaps Mr.
Benson might take me to task on the spot, but not a word
did he say, and during the evening, when I appealed to him
on some musical point, or asked him some questions concerning their customs, his answers, given with an almost
timid, downcast look, were in a subdued and most respect-
ful tone of voice. To say that I was astonished is to put it
mildly. Could this be the man who, although kind enough,
had always treated me in his bluff way like a boy? But before the evening was out I had a glimmering of his purpose,
and after all were gone I was not left in the least doubt.
First he looked carefully around to see that no one was in
sight or hearing, and then went through a list of my short-
comings in his off-hand, decided way. First, I was behind
time in beginning—how was I to expect promptness on the
part of the choir if I was not prompt myself?—then there
was this fault and that fault in the singing that I did not
correct; and he did not believe my making the choir laugh
now and then would wear well in the long run, etc. I have
often been thankful that I did not resent these criticisms,

for, although I did not always take his advice, I received much help from him in the months that followed, and his personal example of subordination and ready obedience in the choir was invaluable in getting it into order.

After I had been at Bowdoin street a few months, Mr. Jacob Abbott, on one of his visits to Boston, asked if he could go with me to one of my class singing lessons. Yes, he could go to one of the public school lessons or to an evening class of ladies and gentlemen. I think he went to both, but remember particularly his visit to the evening class. I knew that he was a great educator, and that his " Mt. Vernon School for Young Ladies " in Boston had been famous a few years before. Mr. Mason taught in it (before the public school work began), and, when one of the young ladies died, composed a tune for the hymn " Sister, Thou wast Mild and Lovely," which was written for the occasion, and called it " Mt. Vernon." I think both hymn and tune are well known now. I was very glad when Mr. Abbott seemed pleased with my classes and my teaching, but had no idea what that approval would lead to. I found out soon after, however. He and his brothers, John S. C., Gorham and Charles, had just started a young ladies' school in New York City, and he wrote them that he thought he had found the teacher they wanted for the music of their institution. Upon their answering, Mr. Jacob spoke to me on the subject of going there. I hesitated; I was doing well, had a large circle of good friends, was near my old home, etc., but Mr. Abbott said: " There is a great field in New York— nothing like Mr. Mason's work and yours has been done there. Here Mr. Mason and Mr. Webb are at the head, and you must for a long time occupy a subordinate place. There you will have a clear field, and I think you can sustain yourself in it. We want such work as you can do in our school, and we think other institutions will want the same when they know what it is." He offered a generous price for a daily class lesson five days in the week, I to have the entire amount I could make from private instruction. He thought, also, that at Mercer Street Church—Dr. Skinner's —where he attended church, they were considering a change, and he believed they would like our kind of large choir. After talking with the folks at home and my good friends in Boston about the matter, I finally said : " If the church position can be secured, I will go." " Well, come and stay a few days with us, and let the people see and hear you, and we believe it will be brought about." I went, gave a lesson or two to the young ladies in class assembled, talked with the church people, played the organ a little, and, at a company assembled at Mr. Abbott's for the purpose, sang my repertoire of songs from Russell's " Ivy Green " to Schubert's " Wanderer." The next day the matter was settled for church and school, and I went back to Boston to arrange for a speedy commencement of my work in the great city of New York. It was some time in 1844 that I left Boston for my new field of labor.

CHAPTER IV.

1844–1847, NEW YORK—ABBOTT'S SCHOOL FOR YOUNG LADIES
—RUTGERS FEMALE INSTITUTE—MISS HAINES' SCHOOL—
THE UNION THEOLOGICAL SEMINARY—THE NEW YORK
INSTITUTION FOR THE BLIND AND THE MERCER ST. PRES-
BYTERIAN CHURCH—MY MARRIAGE—MY QUARTET AND
PERFORMANCE AT THE PHILHARMONIC—SUMMER CONVEN-
TION WORK WITH MESSRS. MASON AND WEBB—MR. JACOB
ABBOTT'S ADVICE ABOUT THE WAY TO KEEP A DIARY.

ABBOTT'S school for young ladies at that time was in
one of the fine houses in the white marble row in La-
fayette Place, New York, spacious and convenient beyond
anything I had before seen. I found the work delightful.
Our methods were new, as Mr. Abbott had said they would
be, and no one having made class teaching and singing te-
dious and unpopular in the school it was not difficult to
arouse and keep up an interest in the lessons. We had frequent visitors—parents and friends of the young ladies, and
other persons interested in seeing the new work, and later
on in hearing the pleasant part-singing. This singing in
parts came along astonishingly soon, for three-quarters of an
hour every school day with those bright, interested girls was
very different from the two half hours a week that I had
been accustomed to in the Public Schools of Boston.

The work had been going on but a few weeks when I
observed one day a large, benignant-looking old gentleman,
accompanied by two younger men, looking on and apparently taking an unusual interest in the lesson I was giving.
This was Dr. Isaac Ferris, then pastor of Rutgers Street

Church, and President of the Board of Trustees of Rutgers Female Institute, and afterward Chancellor of the New York University, and two of the Rutgers Institute trustees. They came to see if the new Yankee music teacher would do for their celebrated old Knickerbocker institution, of which Prof. Charles E. West, LL. D., was then Principal. The result was that I soon added a daily lesson at Rutgers to my work. This institution then occupied a large, commodious building on Madison street, which had been erected for its use. Here I met four hundred girls and young ladies five days in the week, giving three-quarters of an hour at each session. Of my ten years' work in this institution I shall have frequent occasion to speak, as my story goes on.

My duties at Mercer Street Church commenced very soon after my arrival in New York. The chapel of the church was just back of the main building, and facing on Greene street. Here were lecture room and Sunday-school rooms; and over the main entrance a fine octagonal room, which had been especially prepared as a study for the pastor, but Dr. Skinner preferred his home study, which was next door, and this most convenient room for my purposes was turned over to me. I met the choir every Saturday night in the lecture room, but heard individual voices and gave some private lessons in this smaller room, which was my pleasant musical home during my entire New York life.

I remember well my first lesson at a pupil's home in New York. She was one of the young ladies of the Abbott School, and lived on University Place near Twelfth street. I mention it because it will seem strange to those who know New York now, that this point should even then have been so far " up town." I was a few minutes too early when I reached the house, and thought I would walk on to an opening I saw ahead at Fourteenth street. It was rough ground where Union Square now is, and only scattered houses and

blocks around and beyond. A further showing of the great
change in New York since those days is seen in the fact that
Miss Haines' celebrated School for Young Ladies, in which
I commenced teaching soon after, was then on Chambers
street near Broadway. It was some years after that that
Mason Brothers moved from Park Row to Duane street,
because they needed larger quarters, and could get a large
building there at a very low rent, because it was so far up
town, and so near the residence portion of the city. The
business sagacity of the house was, however, shown there as
it was in many other " moves " in following years. They
had a long lease, and sold the balance of it for a good sized
fortune after they had occupied the place two or three years.

In my choir were some students of the Union Theological Seminary, then near by, on University Place, between
Eighth street and Waverly Place. Two of the names, Jes-
sup and Harding, are known to all persons interested in
foreign missions, those men having been at the head of missionary work in India for many years. In due time it was
brought about that I should give two lessons a week to the
students in the Seminary, and the year after I commenced
daily class lessons in the New York State Institution for the
Blind. This establishment occupied a large, fine building
facing Ninth avenue, and owned the entire block of ground
between Thirty-second and Thirty-third streets, and Eighth
and Ninth avenues, then far up town. In walking over
from Twenty-fourth street and Fourth avenue, as I sometimes did, I crossed corn and potato fields, and remember
occasionally being much disgusted at soiling my clean shoes
in a muddy ditch where Madison Square now is.

Within six weeks after the commencement of my work
in New York I was fully occupied. I had not all the class
teaching then that came to me afterward, but all my spare
time was filled with private lessons. As the class-work increased I turned the private lessons over to others.

In Mr. Mason's choir in Boston were several members of
a very musical family by the name of Woodman. One of the
sons, Mr. J. C. Woodman, had a fine baritone voice, and was
one of the soloists in the Boston Academy of Music. He
was a teacher of music, and, as I have mentioned, was Mr.
Mason's first assistant in the introduction of music into
the Public Schools of Boston. He was also a good composer and organist. He is the author of "State Street,"
which, according to the law of "the survival of the fittest,"
has come down to us with the tunes which are still the
standards in our churches where worship, and not musical
display, is the object. His son, R. Huntington Woodman,
of Brooklyn, N. Y., is now one of the most promising young
organists of this or any other country, having recently received endorsements to that effect from the highest musical
authorities of London and Paris, where he played in 1888.

Within a year after I went to New York (in August,
1845) I married J. C. Woodman's sister, Mary Olive. She
was an accomplished singer, and if my children inherit musical qualities they get quite as much from her side of the
house as from mine.

During my first winter at Mercer Street Church I often
said to the officers of the church that I could make the choir
much better if they would have the key-board of the organ
brought out to the front of the gallery so that the choir
could be before me (between me and the organ), instead of
behind me while I was playing—that my voice would help
more, and my directions be better understood and observed,
if I could see all the choir and they could see me. I also
suggested that while they were about it they might make
some much-needed improvement in the organ itself. This
was done the next summer. A judicious expenditure of
two thousand dollars made a great change in the fine old instrument. I was married during the vacation, and when I

returned and put the new soprano and the other leading voices in front of me, with the remaining members of the choir, thirty or forty in number, at their sides, but all in sight, I felt like a king upon his throne, certain of his ability to control and take care of his entire kingdom.

And now my sisters came along, one after another, and went to school either at Rutgers or Abbott's, and under greater advantages pursued their musical studies.   My brother, of whom I have previously spoken, and Mr. Henry T. Lincoln, a noble base, who began his musical career in my first singing school at the " North End " in Boston, in '39, also came, both to sing in my choir and to assist me in my teaching.   A little later my youngest brother, William A. Root, also came, and went to a commercial school and then into a business office.   One of my sisters had an excellent contralto voice, and we now had a well-balanced home quartet—wife, sister, brother and self, and adding Mr. Lincoln, a good quintet.   We took great delight in practicing some of the Mendelssohn part-songs, then comparatively new, and such old madrigals and glees as were set for soprano, alto, tenor, baritone and base.   William Mason, then a very young man, had written a serenade, entitled " Slumber Sweetly, Dearest," that we greatly delighted in. (See page 228.)

After a while we found we were singing with a balance and blending sometimes heard in very simple music by such singers as the Hutchinson family (then in the zenith of their success), but rarely if ever (in our experience) in music of a higher grade, and this encouraged me to strive for the highest perfection possible in every point that I could think of for my quartet.   In one of our summer vacations we all went to the old home in North Reading, and practiced together every day for six weeks—some days hours at a time on a repertoire of about five numbers.   At last I, who was the leader, had no more to think of the others while we were singing together than if I had been singing alone. I could carry out every conception I had in the way of expression —increasing, diminishing, accelerating or retarding, sudden attack or delicate shading, with the utmost freedom, being sure that all would go exactly with me. I had for some time been feeling that a musical demonstration might have to be made in New York, and on their own ground, musically, to some of the chronic contemners of simple music, and of our New England way of teaching it. I knew that as soloists none of us would be regarded as anything more than mediocre, but I believed that as a quartet, with the work we had done, we should at least close their mouths as to our musical competency.

Fortunately, at the previous Commencement of the Rutgers Female Institute, Theodor Eisfeld, the then conductor of the New York Philharmonic Society—the most important musical association in the country—was one of a committee of three to examine the singing class. He pronounced the work good, and so reported. So, soon after the autumn work commenced, I asked Mr. Eisfeld to come and hear us sing a quartet. He was evidently not at all elated by the musical prospect before him, but he was good-natured and came. We began with Mendelssohn's "Hunting Song." Perhaps it was because of his surprise, but his praises were extravagant; so much so that I will not repeat them here. We sang other quartets at his request, and then came the invitation that I had been working for: "Will you sing two numbers at the next Philharmonic concert?" "Oh, yes, with pleasure," and we did. We sang the "Hunting Song" and Wm. Mason's "Serenade." We were somewhat abashed on that occasion at the first sound of our voices—it was such a musical atmosphere as we had never been in before as performers, but we soon pulled ourselves together, and when at the end of the first quartet the musicians of the orchestra laid down their instruments and joined the audience in hearty applause we knew our object had been accomplished. The "Serenade" was encored, and the next day the papers said only pleasant things of our performances. We heard nothing more, in a disagreeable way, about the Yankee singing master. We had passed the ordeal successfully at the highest musical tribunal, and that ended the matter. From that time on I had the good will and friendship of the best musicians in New York, to the end of my stay in that city.

The summer vacations in New York were longer than those of Boston, so I could continue my connection with the great Teachers' Classes of the Boston Academy of Music and of similar gatherings under the direction of Messrs. Mason and Webb in other parts of the country. This was from 1845 onward. It was also a great delight to go with Mr. Mason, when I could, to the day school Teachers' Institutes, which were conducted by Horace Mann and other great educators of that day. They prized Mr. Mason's lessons exceedingly. Mr. Mann said he would walk fifty miles to see Mr. Mason teach if he could not otherwise have that advantage.

That work helped me greatly, for there the principles of teaching as an art were more clearly set forth than they were in our musical work. Once, I remember, at an Institute in Chelsea near Boston I had the pleasure of seeing and hearing Louis Agassiz, the great naturalist—the man who never forgot anything that he had once seen from a beetle to a human being. He was one of the model teachers on that occasion, and it was beautiful to see the facility and accuracy with which he drew upon the blackboard every kind of insect of which he spoke, and most interesting and instructive to listen to his clear Pestalozzian teaching in regard to them. I met him but for a moment as a hundred others did at that

time, but many years after, on being presented to him in a
literary gathering in Chicago, he said, "Ah, I have met you
before—at an Institute in Chelsea, I think." This is mentioned only to illustrate one faculty possessed by that great
man, the extent of which may not be generally known.

Rochester, N. Y., was a favorite place for a week or ten
days' musical convention right after the Boston meeting.
The vocal training class had succeeded so well that they
decided to try harmony, and Mr. Johnson went along for
that. I remember one lovely summer day when we were
thirty or forty miles from Auburn on our way to Rochester,
that we found ourselves almost the only occupants of a large
car. The windows were open to the sweet air of the harvest
fields and we were enjoying to the full the change from the
hot and dusty city to this lovely country. Presently at a
station an hour or so from Auburn, fifteen or twenty young
ladies, evidently all acquainted with each other, entered, and
seated themselves around us. They were in an unusually
merry mood and after awhile began to sing. Their selections were all from the Boston Glee Book, by Messrs. Mason
and Webb, and were sung from memory. We also knew
every piece, and I felt inclined to join, but Mr. Mason looked
dignified, and Mr. Webb, I feared, might not think it quite
proper, so I kept silent, but when they began Mornington's
Glee, "Here in cool grot," Mr. Mason and I evidently
thought of the same thing at the same time—"what will
they do when that bit of base solo comes in?" A glance
from him was sufficient, and when the time came I supplied
it:—"Nor yet for artful strains we call," then Mr. Johnson
joined, and, I think, the older gentlemen assisted, so that
before the glee was through there was quite a little chorus
effect. The young ladies were evidently astonished, but as
evidently pleased. They said nothing to us, nor we to them,
but went on singing, and we continued to supply some tenor

and base. At last Mr. Johnson said to the young lady near-est to him, " Do you know who those two gentlemen are ? " She answered that she did not. " Well, they are Lowell Mason and George James Webb, the authors of the book you have been singing from." That was to her a tremen-dous piece of information. The young singers of the coun-try then regarded those two men as most exalted beings. Almost the only books used were theirs, and their influence and fame were unbounded. The word flew from one to another and not another note was sung. Presently one of the older ones explained to Mr. Webb that they were all attending a young ladies' school in Auburn, and two or three hours before had come in a body to the station at Auburn to to see a school-mate off, and that the conductor had invited them to take this ride, and now they were returning. I remember that we did not go on from Auburn until the next morning (there was no thought of sleeping cars in those days), and that, at this young lady's invitation, Mr. Webb and I called upon her at her father's house in the evening.

My Quintet went once during a summer vacation with Mr. Johnson on a short convention tour into New York State, and that was about the last of both Quartet and Quin-tet for concert singing, for my sister became engaged to a New York gentleman who objected to that sort of publicity for her. Once I remember that I so far overcame his scruples that he gave his consent to her singing at a concert that Gottschalk was to give in Dodworth's Hall, but when the time came she was too ill to sing and some other perform-ance took our place. I mention it because we were to sing there a quartet that Mr. Eisfeld composed for us soon after our advent at the Philharmonic, and which we had sung, I think, at one of his chamber concerts, and with great delight in our practice and to friends. It begins, " On the lake's unruffled surface," and I presume may still be found. It will repay careful study. (See page 229.)

I ought to say something more here of that remarkable family with whom it was my good fortune to be connected during my ten years in New York. The published works of Jacob Abbott and of John S. C. Abbott are known. In the legal profession the works of Benjamin Vaughan Abbott and of Austin Abbott are, I am told, regarded as standards, and in the theological and editorial world Lyman Abbott is one of the most eminent men of the present time. These three last mentioned are sons of Jacob Abbott, and were boys at the time of which I write. That, however, which is not " known and read of all " is the home and school-life of these admirable men. In their homes and in their school-rooms, with each other and with all who were connected with them, either as pupils or teachers, their intercourse was characterized by a sincerity and a gentle friendliness so steady and so constant that breaking over it into roughness of any kind or into disobedience seemed impossible. I saw no outbreak or case of " discipline " in all the years that I was with them. That their excellent methods and great skill and attainments as teachers had something to do with the result will of course be understood. They were called in the school by no other names than " Mr. Jacob," " Mr. John," " Mr. Gorham," and " Mr. Charles," and I was always " Mr. George," and my brother " Mr. Towner."

As larger buildings were needed the school was moved, first to Houston street, then to Bleecker, both near Broadway. I can not remember just when the brothers decided to have two schools, and now I miss my diary again. In fact, as I go on, I miss it more and more. That book, by the way, and the circumstances that caused it, are worth speaking of.

Early in my New York life Mr. Jacob said to me one day: " Did you ever keep a diary?" "Yes," I answered, "I have begun a half dozen at least." "You haven't any of them now?" "No." "You burned each one after writing a few weeks or a few months in it." "Yes." "Was it because you had been so sentimental that you gradually grew tired of what you had written, and at last ashamed to have any one see it?" I laughed and said it was exactly so. "Well," he said, "that is a very common experience. I will tell you what kind of a diary you will never wish to burn. Get a good sized, substantially bound blank-book and record in it simply facts of your every-day life; first, every event of your past life, with its date, that you think you would like to remember years hence, then begin where you are now and do the same thing every day. Speak of pupils, letters, people you see, concerts, classes, journeys—in short, every occurrence of any prominence that is connected with your work or home. Do not give an opinion or admit a word of sentiment in regard to any of the records you make, but let them be stated in the briefest and most concise manner possible. They may look dry to you now, but years hence they will be full of associations of the successful and pleasant life you are now living, and instead of growing tiresome as you read them, they will become more and more interesting and valuable."

I saw at once how good this advice was, and went right off to Mr. Ivison (who was then a member of Mercer Street choir) and had the book made. It was as large as a good-sized ledger, was bound in strong leather, and so arranged that it could be locked. As soon as it was done I asked Mr. Jacob to come and see it. He came, and when he had looked and approved I asked him to begin it for me. He did, and this is about what he wrote:

"Mr. George has brought me in here to see his new book. This is his music room. It is octagonal in shape, two corners being cut off for closets and two for doors of entrance. The wood-work is oak. An octagonal table occupies the center, and book-cases with glass doors are on the side between the doors. There is a piano and a lounge here, and several easy chairs in convenient places. Twenty years hence, Mr. George, when you read this in some totally different scene let it remind you of your New York music room and

"MR. JACOB."

I did as he advised—began with my early life, and found I could recall almost everything of importance before going to Boston, and while there, then started from that time (early in 1845) to make short daily records. This went through my New York life, my first stay in Europe, and my early convention work to 1871, when we were in full tide of successful business in Chicago—more than twenty-five years of brief, close record. The book was but little more than half full, and how true were Mr. Jacob's ideas about the memories and associations it recalled. "Closing exercises at Rutgers to-day" was not merely the record of a musical exercise twenty years before. About that commonplace event were now summer flowers, bright skies and dear friends— and the flowers grew sweeter, the skies brighter, and the friends dearer as the years rolled on. But a memorable day came when my big journal shared the fate of its little predecessors. It was burned! But not by my hand. It went up, with many other mementos of my former life, in the flames of the great Chicago fire.

Somebody may be as much obliged to me as I was to Mr. Jacob for this suggestion about the way to keep a diary.

CHAPTER V.

1848–1849, NEW YORK—SPINGLER INSTITUTE—ADDING DIFFI-
CULTIES TO THE MUSICAL WORK OF MY CLASSES—REFER-
ENCE TO DR. MASON'S FIRST "SINGING SCHOOL"—MY
FIRST EFFORTS AT COMPOSITION AND BOOK-MAKING—
DIFFERENT MUSICAL GRADES—JENNY LIND.

IT must have been about 1848 that the heirs of the Spingler estate in New York city erected a fine stone building
on Union Square, between Fourteenth and Fifteenth streets,
for Mr. Gorham Abbott's school. On the corner of Fifteenth
street, where Tiffany now is, had already been built a large
church for Dr. Cheever. Mr. Gorham Abbott's school was
called the "Spingler Institute," and the church was called
the "Church of the Puritans." Mr. Spingler was a dairy-
man, who some years before had kept his cows thereabout.
His little farm took in some acres from where Union Square
now is, to near Sixth avenue, and from Fourteenth street
upward a block or two.

People were disposed to be humorous about the name
" Spingler " at first. It was suggested that " Spinster Institute " would be more appropriate, but the result was a good
illustration of the fact that a name, whether of a person, or
a town, or a street, or an institute, takes on the character of
what it names. If that is excellent or beautiful, the name
soon becomes so to those interested, however lacking it may
be in euphony or beauty in the abstract. " Spingler " soon
lost its odd sound to us and came to be just the word to
mean an elegant structure, fitted in a costly manner for its
purposes, and filled with young ladies of culture and refinement.

Mr. Abbott was constantly adding to the attractiveness of the institution by various means. One of his most important purchases was the original " Voyage of Life," by Thomas Cole—four large pictures—which he hung on the walls of the Chapel where the daily singing lessons were given, and where were enjoyed many fine concerts and literary entertainments.

Connected with the Abbott school I often think of a bright, vivacious girl, who was always conspicuous in the school entertainments, especially in those that had any fun in them. She was an excellent scholar and a great favorite. This was Helen Fiske, now known the world over as Helen Hunt Jackson (H. H.).

One of the first troubles that I met in the classes at Rutgers and Abbott's was that the course which took the whole year in the Boston public schools here lasted but a couple of months, the difference being between two half-hour lessons a week to children, and daily lessons of three-quarters of an hour to young ladies and bright, interested girls. When I saw the end of my usual course approaching I did not know exactly what to do for exercises, but finally decided to work in the more remote keys, major and minor (from the blackboard), and to have the class transpose the scales, both major and harmonic minor, through all the keys. Understand, when I say transpose the *scales* I mean just that. Singing one exercise or tune in one key, and then a different exercise or tune in another, is not transposing the scale—it is not transposition at all. What my classes did was to sing the scale in the key of C, ascending and descending, and then the same in G, then in D, and so on through the enharmonic change from the key of F-sharp to the key of G-flat, back to the key of C—out through the sharps (so to speak), and back through the flats, or *vice versa*. First the major scales, then the minor, then each major, followed by its rela-

tive minor in a series, as, C, A, G, E, D, B, etc. I thought
this for exercise practice would occupy the year, but it did
not take three months to do the work well, without an instrument, and to read pretty difficult diatonic lessons in all
the keys, major and minor. Then I began upon the practice of the chromatic scale, feeling sure that that would last
through the term, but it did not. In two months, or thereabout, the classes at Rutgers and Spingler could sing that
series in any key to syllables, or "la," or "ah," rapidly and
accurately. All this is not wonderful now, but it was then.
At the annual examinations of the classes at Rutgers three
of the best musicians of the city were regularly chosen to
pass upon the work, and the Principal and Trustees of the
Institute, and all concerned, greatly enjoyed their surprise
and unlimited praise.

About the time we had accomplished the work of singing
the chromatic scale, as above described, I had occasion to go
to Boston for a day, and told Mr. Mason what we had done.
"What! four hundred girls sing the chromatic scale in the
way you describe? I can't believe it." I assured him that
it was so, but left him in evident doubt. At the next summer vacation, when we met for the usual Teacher's Class
and Convention work, he said " That chromatic scale singing
is not so difficult after all. I have tried it in one of the
schools here, and they do it fairly well already." I make
this record in the belief that the musical exercises above described were the first ever undertaken in class-teaching in
this country.

If this seems strange, it must be remembered that we
were then in the early times of class-teaching as we know it
now. It was not many years before that Wm. C. Woodbridge (who may be remembered as the author of a once
popular geography and atlas) called Mr. Mason's attention
to Nageli & Pfeiffer's method of adapting Pestalozzi's idea of

teaching to vocal music. Mr. Mason liked what he could
see of it very much ; then Mr. Woodbridge said to him : " If
you will call together a class I will translate and write out
each lesson for you (the work was in German) as you want
it, and you can try the method; it will take about twenty-
four evenings." This was done, and the class was held in
the large lecture room of Park Street Church, Boston. Dr.
Mason has often described how he took Mr. Woodbridge's
translation in one hand and his pointer in the other, and developed, as well as he could, what was afterward embodied
in the " Teacher's Manual of the Boston Academy of Music,"
as the Pestalozzian method of teaching vocal music in
classes. The class was composed largely of prominent people of the city who were interested in musical education, and
all were greatly delighted with the new way.

That was undoubtedly the first class of its kind ever
taught in the English speaking world, and its essential principles exist now wherever the ideas of key relationship and
the movable " do" prevail. Speaking to Dr. Mason once
about this remarkable class, I asked him what those ladies
and gentleman paid for that course of twenty-four lessons.
" Oh, they arranged that among themselves," he replied.
" They decided that five dollars apiece would be about
right." "And how many were there in the class ? " He
smiled as he answered : "About five hundred."

Up to this time I had not written anything to speak of.
I did put together some simple tunes while in Boston, one
of which (Rosedale) has come along down in a modest way
with its more popular companions, being occasionally sung
and asked for at the present time. After I was well under
way in New York Mr. Bradbury and Mr. Woodbury used to
say : " Root, why don't you make books; we are doing well
in that line,"—but I had no inclination that way. I am
ashamed to say it, but I looked then with some contempt

upon their grade of work. My ladies' classes and choirs were singing higher music, and my blind pupils were exciting the admiration of the best musical people of the city by their performances of a still higher order of compositions. There was a well-balanced choir of sixty good voices in this institution for the blind, and they worked with an interest and enthusiasm that was wonderful to see. We sang, eventually, Romberg's setting of Schiller's "Song of the Bell," "Morning," by Ries, several of Mendelssohn's Part-songs, and several choruses from his and other oratorios. "Thanks be to God, He laveth the thirsty land," from "Elijah," I remember they liked best of all, and sang extremely well.

After a while I began to find it difficult to get proper music for my girls at Rutgers and Spingler to sing, and it took so much time to select what was needed and cost so much to get copies enough, that I felt that something must be done in the way of preparing music especially for them. There was also a strong pressure from classes and teachers —at Rutgers especially—for new music for opening and closing religious exercises. So I got together the material for my first book. It was called "The Young Ladies' Choir." I did not ask anybody to publish it, but just had copies enough made for my own use. I don't think I even copyrighted it, for I had no thought then in regard to composition and book-making beyond supplying my own needs. This book was used two or three years for devotional exercises, but its secular music lasted but a few months, and then my brother and I began the plan of getting up pamphlets of such music as I needed, still seeking no publisher, and thinking only of my own wants. At this time, too, I began to write and arrange music for my choir in the same way, only I did not need so many copies, and so did not go to the expense of having it printed. I had manuscript books for each part, and had each part copied in, or, if I found something printed that I liked, had it cut out and pasted in.

The first book that I had anything to do with that
sought a publisher was made with and at the suggestion of
the organist of Dr. Cheever's church, then on the corner of
Fifteenth street and Broadway, J. E. Sweetser. It was called
" Root & Sweetser's Collection." It contained the music we
had been gathering for our choirs, with such other material
as we could collect and purchase, and an elementary department which, for scientific but uninteresting exercises, could
not be excelled; they were taken largely from elementary
works that Hullah was then using in England. A few
choirs adopted the book, and some of the music is still sung;
but, as a whole, it was not at all adapted for popular use.
I did not then realize what people in elementary musical
states needed.

How true it is that to every music lover and learner
there is a grade of music in which he lives, so to speak—
where he feels most at home and enjoys himself best. When
he hears or studies music that is above that grade, if he is
sensible he simply says : " That is above me ; I am not there
yet." If he is not sensible, he is liable to say : " There's no
music in that." The conversation of two gentlemen at one
of our recent Thomas concerts is a good illustration of that
condition of things. One says: " Do you call that music? "
The other answers : " Yes; and the best there is—it is a
composition by Wagner." To which his friend responds :
" Well, for my part, I think Wagner had better stick to his
sleeping cars, and let music alone."

People change their musical homes, or rather add to
them, as they progress in musical appreciation. At first
they care only for the little way-side flowers and simple
scenery of the land of tonic, dominant and subdominant.
They regard the musical world outside of that boundary as
a kind of desert, entirely unfit to live in, and I may add once
more, what has often been said in substance, that many

people remain in this musical condition all their lives. But those who progress, begin, by and by, to see some beauty in the sturdier growths and the more varied scenery, and after awhile realize that the still unexplored regions beyond may be yet more beautiful when they are reached.

But here there is a danger. People in this state are apt to grow conceited, and to despise the simple conditions they once enjoyed. "Unworthy, narrow and bigoted" are the proper terms to apply to such. The way-side flower has its place in the economy of God's creation as truly as the oak, and the little hill and the brooklet are as truly beautiful as the mountain and torrent are grand.

"But," some one says, "there is so much trash in the simple music of the day." There is trash at every musical grade, even to the highest. How much that is grotesque and senseless is seen in the ambitious attempts of those who follow Wagner, or would rival him in new paths, but have nothing of his transcendent genius. Such are usually among the despisers of the elementary conditions through which all must pass, and in which a majority of the music-loving world must always be. "Trash" of course; so there are offensive plants and flowers and disagreeable scenes, but the proportion is small, and I contend that most of the simple music that *lives* is no more trash than Mozart's "O dolce concento" or "Rousseau's Dream," than which nothing is written that is simpler or more perfect.

In returning to my story I must not omit to speak of the great musical sensation of 1849—the advent of Jenny Lind. P. T. Barnum had engaged her for a certain number of concerts in this country at what was then considered an enormous price. With consummate skill he had seized upon the fine reputation which she had among musicians and extended it among all the people. He manufactured and manipulated public opinion until the excitement was intense.

An angel could not have met the expectation he raised in many minds.

There was then no hall in New York large enough to hold the people that wanted to see this wonderful being on the occasion of her first concert, so Castle Garden was prepared. I think it was arranged to seat about ten thousand people. Even then the lowest priced seats were in the neighborhood of three dollars, if I remember rightly, and a large sum was realized by selling the choice of seats at auction. An enterprising hatter, by the name of Genin, captured fame and fortune by paying six hundred dollars for first choice.

What a breathless hush rested upon the vast audience when the time came for her first song, and what a burst of welcome greeted her swift coming forward. She was simply dressed in white, and was most statuesque in her apparent calmness as she waited for the orchestra to finish the prelude to "Casta Diva." It was daring in her, under the circumstances, to risk a first impression on the long, soft tone with which that aria commences, but it was a great success. While you wondered at its extreme pianissimo you were distinctly conscious that its fine, steady intensity penetrated to the remotest corner of the hall. All were filled with wonder and delight, excepting those victims of the great advertiser, who were bound to be disappointed if her tones were anything like those of a human being.

She had a long and very successful career in this country, making a large fortune for herself and a much larger one for her enterprising manager. A small financial transaction of my own, in connection with her concerts, comes freshly to my mind with a good deal of satisfaction. I thought I was commissioned to get a lot of tickets for one of the schools, but it proved I was not, and the tickets were on my hands—about twenty, if I remember rightly. But I "speculated" with them, and made money enough by the operation to pay for all my Jenny Lind concerts. I heard her first note and her last, both in Castle Garden, and spent nearly nine months abroad between them.

CHAPTER VI.

ABOUT this time I began to feel the effects of my reckless treatment of a naturally strong and healthy constitution. For years I took a hasty breakfast before other people were up, in order to be with my blind class, nearly two miles off, at half past seven in the morning. Then every working hour through the day was filled with other classes and private lessons, and some nights in the week with evening work, and if a new pupil wanted my dinner hour I gave it and snatched a lunch as I could get it in place of the regular meal. This, with the Sunday work, gradually sapped my vitality and brought on the usual trouble of overworked people—dyspepsia.

I think it was early in November of 1850 that Mr. Jacob Abbott said to me one day, "Mr. George, you should stop work for a while. Go to Paris. (He made nothing of picking up his satchel and going across, writing on his books during the voyage, and while there.) The trip will do you good, and Paris is a good place to rest and amuse yourself in, and, if you feel like it when you get there, you can study the language and anything more about music that you wish to know; for the best teachers of the world congregate there." My wife was considerably astonished when I told her what Mr. Jacob had said, and that I believed I should go. However, she agreed that if it could be managed it would be a good plan.

The first thing was to see how the church people would feel about it, and how the organ and choir could be attended to during my absence. This was soon ascertained and settled. One of the elders of the church and the chairman of the music committee was John P. Crosby, an older brother of the present Dr. Howard Crosby. He was one of the noblest gentlemen I have ever known, and one of the truest and dearest friends I ever had. He was very musical —entirely competent to teach the choir and play the organ, and in a day or two after I told him my plan I was not surprised when he said: "It is all arranged. Leave Mrs. Root to be our leader, and I'll meet the choir and play the organ for you until you return, and your salary shall go on all the same." I ought to have said that there was no thought of my wife's going with me, partly because that would have been too great a strain on our finances, but more, perhaps, because we then had two little children, F. W., four years old, and Charlie, three years younger.

I engaged Richard Storrs Willis (a brother of N. P. Willis, an author of considerable celebrity in those days) to teach for me at Rutgers and Spingler Institutes, and Sigismund Lasar to carry on the work at the Institution for the Blind during my absence. Much of my work would naturally have fallen to my brother, but he had a little while before accepted an offer to teach for the winter in Alabama. I took my passage for the fifth of December, 1850, on the Franklin, a new steamer of a new line just established between New York and Havre, and then went to Boston and to the old home to say good-bye. A few days before sailing I decided to get my life insured. I mention it because it was one of the early risks of the " N. Y. Mutual

Life," now the largest institution of the kind in the world. When I see their present magnificent building I contrast it mentally with the little office in Wall street where I arranged to have a certain moderate sum paid to my wife in case of my death. Although not a large amount it has improved considerably since that day, more than forty years ago.

The " Splendid Steamer Franklin " was a small affair in comparison with the present ocean liners, but, notwithstanding she bowed and rolled as gracefully as she could at every wave of that wintry sea, and made nearly all of us very seasick, she carried us safely across and landed us in due time (thirteen days, I think) at Havre. I had some letters which enabled me to settle myself pleasantly in Paris almost immediately on my arrival.

One of my plans was to learn as much of the language as possible while there, and I asked a son of my landlady— a young collegian who could speak English a little—if he would give me lessons. He was timid and hesitated about undertaking it, but I told him he would not have any responsibility; that I would be the teacher and he would have only to obey orders. He agreed, and I commenced with the then popular " Ollendorf."

I had seen a good deal of the teaching of French in the schools in New York, and thought I saw why so few learners were willing to try to speak even short phrases in that language. They were like piano pupils, who know how their exercises ought to go, but can not make the proper movements of their fingers at the proper time—they have continually to stop or stumble for want of muscular control, which simply means want of practice.

I saw that in French there were new adjustments of the vocal and articulating organs for certain sounds which are not in our own language, and that there were constantly successions of familiar sounds in an entirely new way. It seemed to me also that just as new and difficult successions of finger movements could only be rendered smooth and certain by much repetition and practice, so the new sounds of a strange language could only be made to follow each other fluently by the same means.

So, when my youthful teacher would have passed my imperfect pronunciation and hesitating utterance of a phrase because I had all the words right, I said, " No, we have only begun—have only laid out the work for this phrase; now you say it, and I will say it after you, not only until it goes smoothly and unhesitatingly, but has just the right vowel and consonant sounds." I tired that young man dreadfully, but he was rather proud of his pupil after a while. Only once, I remember, I undertook too much. The phrase was: "*un peu plus haut*" (a little higher), and I said : " Now I am going to repeat that after you until there is no foreign accent in it at all, and you say you could not tell it from a Frenchman." But in vain ; he was too honest, and the exact shades of difference between the vowels of "*peu*" and "*plus*," or some other subtle peculiarity of utterance always caused the same result. " Is it like a Frenchman now?" "*Non, monsieur.*" Again and again I tried. I asked him to show or tell me what caused the difference between his utterance and mine. This he could not do. Each word alone after him he seemed to think right, but when put together it was to his ears a foreigner speaking. All he could say was: "*N'entendez vous pas la différence, monsieur?*" And I had to answer that I did not.

On reflection, I saw that this might be so; for all foreigners who learn our language after they are grown up, although they may have the entire vocabulary, and for practical purposes may speak as well as a native, are still readily perceived to be foreigners. It is only as children, when the organs are tender and can be moulded, that we learn to speak a foreign language without accent.

If an educational word on this subject would not be considered out of place here, I would say to the piano teacher: When your pupil is not willing to play for friends under proper circumstances, it is generally because he is afraid his fingers will not go right, and that he will be mortified by hesitations or blunders at certain places—in short, he does not want to play because he has not practiced enough to get that muscular control which gives confidence. To the teacher of the foreign language I say the same thing. If your pupil is not willing to speak in the language you are teaching him, it is in most cases because the muscles of the articulating organs will not obey his will—he has not practiced his *five-finger exercises* enough, so to speak.

People like to do what they can do well. If they play the piano well, even though the pieces be simple, they like to play to those who enjoy their music; if they speak readily and smoothly in a foreign language they like to exercise their powers in that way, even though they may know but a few phrases and may make many mistakes in construction or grammar. If a piano teacher allows a new exercise or piece before the previous one is perfectly learned, or a French teacher goes on to a second phrase while there is the least hesitation in the utterance of the one at which the pupil is at work, trouble, and, in the end, failure and dissatisfaction will be the certain result.

I studied the language and looked about the city for two or three weeks before commencing the more regular work that occupied me later. The first thing in a musical way that interested me very much was the singing and organ playing at Christmas time in the Church of the Madeleine. A boy with a wonderful voice sang the melody of the "Adeste Fideles" ("Portuguese Hymn," as we know it) at the priests' end of the church, the choir, which was also there, coming in with the ending of each verse, the organ, which was situated with the singers, giving a different harmony with each verse, and then another organ, several times larger, four hundred feet off, over the front entrance, rolled out an interlude between the verses. It was a strange effect to me and very impressive.

About this time I began taking voice lessons. I forget who it was in New York who told me to go to Giulio Alary, but when I got to Paris I found that he was the great man in that line outside of the Conservatoire. It shows how large the world is, and how fast it moves, that perhaps no one who reads this will ever have heard of this man, who was so conspicuous as a composer and teacher a generation ago in Paris and London. I sang a good deal with him from an oratorio of his called "La Redemption," and while I was with him his opera "Les Trois Marriages" was performed at the Italian opera-house there, with Sontag, Lablache, and Gardoni in the cast.

At the close of my lesson one day he said: "I am going to the last rehearsal of my opera. You can come with me and hear these people sing if you like." I was in trouble, for I knew I could not make him conceive how there could be any conscientious scruples against accepting his invitation, but at that time, in the church to which I belonged, it was thought wrong to go to opera or theatrical representations, and I determined when I left home that I would do nothing in Paris that I would not do in New York. So I explained as well as I could why I could not go. He did not understand it at all, as I knew he could not, and evidently regarded me as a kind of fanatic—an opinion in which I coincided a few years later. I never felt quite comfortable with him after that scene, but he soon had to go to London where his opera was next performed, and I went to another teacher.

Jacques Potharst was some kind of a northman by birth, but he had lived in Italy and France nearly all his life, and had been a successful tenor in the Italian Opera. He was a good teacher, and I took lessons of him during the rest of my stay in Paris. One day he said, " I have another American pupil, a baritone, whom you must meet. I have some duets that will just suit your two voices." That was soon brought about. My compatriot proved to be a young man by the name of Mann. He was the son of one of our government officials, who was, in pursuance of his diplomatic duties, sometimes in one European country and sometimes in another. Just then he was living in Paris. Young Mann had an exceptionally fine baritone voice, and we sang together a good deal, not only at our lessons, but in musical companies, where Signor Potharst seemed to take a good deal of pride in parading his American pupils.

This young gentleman was a good illustration of what I was saying about the way to speak a foreign language without accent. His father began his diplomatic career when this son, his only child, was very young—about ten years of age I think. He went to school in every country where they made any stay, and was left long enough in each one to acquire the language. His French, German and Italian were absolutely without foreign accent, as I was told by those who knew. I extend this remembrance of my friend because one of those curious happenings that sometimes take place has brought him freshly to my mind. Last year one of my neighbors said, "I have rented a house on this street for the summer, to a gentleman by the name of Mann, who says that he knows you—that you were together in Paris forty years ago." I called on him, and instead of the slender youth of eighteen, found a portly gentleman of fifty-eight, now Judge Mann, of Florida, who, with his wife, formerly a Chicago lady, was going to pass the sum-

mer by Lake Michigan. I need not say that we renewed
our acquaintance, music and all, with much pleasure.

Before leaving New York a gentleman of my acquaintance said to me, "My daughter will arrive in Paris soon
after you. The family with whom she is going are not musical, and I shall take it as a great favor if you will see that
she has a good piano teacher while she is there. This I
readily undertook to do. By good fortune Gottschalk, the
great pianist, was passing a few months in Paris, and I found
him willing to give some lessons to my young friend, who
already played well for an amateur. This was the beginning
of an acquaintance with that distinguished man, which continued up to that fatal journey to South America, from which
he never returned.

I say *"great* pianist" of L. Moreau Gottschalk advisedly.
Critics and some prominent musicians did not call him a
great player—all agreed that he was an exquisite player,
and all admitted that he was the most popular and successful concert pianist that ever played in America, but those
who knew him well could testify to his wonderful repertoire
of classic music. He could play all of Beethoven by heart,
and he delighted in Bach, but he was too honest to play such
music to any extent at his popular concerts, and too strong
in the consciousness of his own merit to heed those critics
who, if they could have their way, would never give the
people any music that they could understand and enjoy.

It was particularly exasperating to hear unfavorable criticisms of Gottschalk's compositions, for they are not only
understandable and useful to the people, but elegant and
musicianly in a high degree. I think it may be said that
his are among the most original and characteristic of all
American compositions for the piano-forte.

My daily life was now pretty regular. Ollendorf, voice
and piano practice, lessons and recitations until afternoon;

then the picture galleries, museums, libraries, palaces, cathe-
drals, parks, gardens, and endless objects of interest until
five or six o'clock. Then dinner, and afterward gathering
in the parlor for conversation or music. One evening a
week at the Protestant Chapel, where I always went on
Sunday, and occasionally a concert, occupied my time.

Two concerts I remember with special interest: One
was at a small hall connected with Henri Herz's piano
establishment, at which Madame Sontag, Madame Viardot
Garcia, Lablache, and Gardoni, a young tenor of great promise, sang. I do not know that these names will excite the
interest now that they did then, and for some years after,
over the entire musical world. Sontag was the soprano of
her time. Viardot Garcia was not only a great mezzo-so-
prano and accomplished pianist, but being the sister of
Malibran, one of the greatest singers that ever lived, and
then recently deceased, excited great interest wherever she
appeared. But Lablache was the king. He had been the
greatest basso of the world for a quarter of a century or
more. He was a giant in size, his magnificent head crowned
with a thick mass of white hair, towering far above his
companions as they stood together upon the stage. It had
been my greatest desire for years to hear this man, whose
fame was greater then than that which any singer enjoys
now, that I know of. His voice was proportionate to his
size, and had the advantage of being trumpet-toned like a
tenor, or rolling out like the sub-base of an organ, at his
pleasure. It was said that at C-sharp or D above, no orchestra, however large, could be more than a fair accompaniment
when he chose to put forth all his power, and I could readily
believe it. I heard his D-flat below, in a concerted number
in which all joined, and the ponderous solidity of the long-
sustained tone could only be compared to a grand sub-base,
though it was much richer in quality than any instrument
could produce.

Madame Viardot played a difficult waltz by Chopin, to which had been added, in a most musicianly manner, a melody which she sang. It was a curious and wonderful performance. Madame Sontag and Lablache sang a humorous duet—an Italian singing master giving his favorite pupil a lesson. He was so large and she so *petite* by comparison, that when he nodded his great bushy head in admiring approval of her brilliant execution he brought to mind the old story of the lion who found a congenial companion in a canary bird.

I came near meeting this great man once, but, much to my regret, did not quite succeed. It was while I was taking lessons from M. Alary. He was one day looking for a song that he wished me to practice, when at last he said, "now I remember; Lablache has it; I will send for it." I asked him to let me call for it on my way home, and he readily consented. He gave me a note which described what was wanted, and I took it to the great basso's apartments, but he was at dinner. I heard his ponderous voice and jovial laugh in the next room, but did not see him; his daughter brought me the book.

The second concert to which I referred was in the Italian Opera-house. It was Rossini's "Stabat Mater," and was the only occasion while I was in Paris that I entered an opera-house or theater. Sims Reeves came over from London to sing the tenor solos. Down deep in the French heart there is a national animosity to English people, but they could not resist the charm of that performance. At the "Cujus animam" they were wild with delight, and recalled the great tenor again and again.

The first English tenor of this generation is Edward Lloyd. In the last generation Sims Reeves was the acknowledged best, and in the generation before, Braham. When, therefore, at a recent Musical Festival in Cincinnati

(May, 1888), I heard Lloyd, I had heard the three great tenors of the three generations, and what greatly increased the interest of this fact was, that I heard Braham sing Handel's "Sound an alarm," Sims Reeves the "Cujus animam," and Edward Lloyd both of those songs.

Two other concerts I now remember that are perhaps worth mentioning. At one was a new composition by Felicien David, conducted by himself. I forget what it was, but at that time he was very famous as the composer of "The Desert," a kind of cantata, founded largely upon Arabian melodies. The new piece was good, but not striking, and verified what Auber was reported as having said: "When David descends from his camel you will find he is not at all remarkable." But what was more especially in my mind when I began to speak of that concert was the performance on that occasion of the "Hallelujah chorus." It was so fast as to be ridiculous. Colossus had lost all his dignity and strength by crossing the channel.

The other concert that I think of with special interest was an orchestral performance of new compositions by Hector Berlioz, conducted by himself. That pale, wild face, surmounted by shaggy locks, black as night, haunted me for months. He was a disappointed man. His works, now taking so high a rank, did not find much recognition in his life-time.

CHAPTER VII.

1851, PARIS AND LONDON—FOURTH OF JULY—THE CONVERSA-
TIONAL MODE OF LEARNING FRENCH, AND THE ROMANCE
THAT FOLLOWED—TWO CONCERTS AT EXETER HALL, LON-
DON—THE LOYALTY OF THE ENGLISH TO OLD FAVORITES
—THE FIRST WORLD'S EXPOSITION—AMERICAN FRIENDS—
THE M'CORMICK REAPER—THE SEWING MACHINE—THE
DAY & NEWELL LOCK—THE YACHT AMERICA—THE NAR-
ROW ESCAPE ON THE HOME VOYAGE.

MY stay in Paris was just before the famous *coup d'etat*
of Louis Napoleon. He was then simply President,
but there was a half-concealed anxiety in the community
lest they might be on the eve of some outbreak or calamity,
as indeed they were.

When the fourth of July came, six of us Americans
decided to make a day of it in honor of the fatherland. We
went out to Enghien, a pretty suburb a few miles from
Paris, and celebrated in various ways, much to our enjoyment and somewhat to the surprise of the natives. We
came home for dinner at five o'clock, and then adjourned to
the parlor for a grand wind-up. We made speeches and
sang songs—the " Star-Spangled Banner," "America," and
whatever else we could think of that would be appropriate.
At last I started " The Marseillaise "—" Ye sons of freedom,
wake to glory," etc. I had not proceeded far when good
Madame Maffit, our landlady, came rushing in. " O, gentlemen, stop, I beg of you," she said ; " a crowd is collecting
in the street—the *gendarmes* will come—my house will be
ruined ;" and she flew to the windows, which had been

open, and shut them violently. "Oh, we are only celebrating our American Independence," one of us said. "Well, we are not independent enough yet to sing 'The Marseillaise,'" she answered.

That song had been interdicted some time before, and although France was then nominally a Republic, the Government was still afraid of its effect upon that inflammable people. An old officer, who had served under the first Napoleon, and had been decorated by the great Emperor himself, was one of Madame Maffit's boarders. He went down to the street, and in some way induced the crowd to disperse. Our landlady assured us that if we had continued five minutes longer we might have had to make our explanations at the *Prefecture*—an ending to our celebration that we certainly should not have enjoyed.

In pursuance of my plan to improve myself all I could in the French language, I entered into conversation with the natives whenever I had an opportunity. The first Napoleon's old soldiers were always to be found in the parks and gardens on pleasant days. They had nothing to do, and were always ready for a talk as soon as they found I was an American. One word about *Le grand Empereur*, whose memory they worshiped, was enough to see them off, and much practice their garrulous enthusiasm gave me, both in listening to rapid utterances and in framing questions to bring them out.

But my most important opportunities in this way were in the parlor of our *Pension*, where all the household assembled for a while after dinner. I talked a good deal with two sisters from Metz, whose business it was to copy pictures in the Louvre and other galleries, mostly for the churches of the provinces. A pretty romance came from this acquaintance, which is worth relating.

They were intensely interested in all I could tell them

of America, about which their ignorance was surprising.
Was New York in North or South America? was *La Nou-
velle Orleans* near New York? were there many white
people? had we to be constantly on our guard against the
Indians? etc. They were greatly interested in the daguerre-
otypes of my wife and children (there were no photographs
then), and utterly astonished at my description of American
social life. Could it be possible that a young lady could go
to a concert or to the theater alone with a young man, or
receive him at her home without the presence of a third person? Did they decide upon and arrange their marriages
themselves? It seemed incredible. They did not see why
good girls might not do all that, but it would not be thought
of in France. In fact, nice girls in France could not marry
at all unless they had a "portion" (*dot*). Men they would
marry would not have them, and men that would marry
them they would not have. I expatiated upon the self-
reliance of our girls—how young people married when they
fell in love, and of their happy married lives. I grew eloquent in very ungrammatical French on the advantages of
our ways, and volunteered a good deal of information as to
probable results if they were in America instead of in
France. I would think of something to say that I thought
would interest them, and then see if I could say it, not realizing the full signification that it might bear to their
minds. In fact, it did not seem as if the kind of French I
was speaking could mean much of anything, but I should
have been considerably astonished if I could have known
then how I was making America, and especially New York,
appear to them the veritable land of promise. This feeling
grew stronger as we became better acquainted.

I sometimes saw them at their copying in the Louvre,
but, mindful of the proprieties as there regarded, never ac-
costed them while they were at their work. I was not

much of a judge of painting, but what they did seemed to me good. Adèle, the older sister, was exceptionally fine looking, the younger something of an invalid, and the good heart of the former was constantly shown in her tender care of her less favored sister. I admired Adèle greatly, and if I thought of some sentence like "I think you would do well in your profession in New York," or, "You would not be long in America without marrying," I would say it as best I could, thinking mainly of its construction and very little of its meaning ; and this was not insincerity—what I said was true enough, but I should have made some further modification of my sentences if I could have foreseen what they would lead to.

To finish this little story I shall have to transfer the scene to New York, then I will return and finish the account of my Paris visit. I had not been long at home when the *coup d'etat* took place. A few weeks after that I received a letter from Adèle, saying that they had lost nearly all their little property, and that there was then nothing for them to do in France—that their only hope now was America, which, from my representation, was exactly the place for them to go to. She said she should go first alone, and when she had established herself, her sister would join her. She wrote to me because I was the only person in America that she knew—would write again when she had decided what ship to go in, and then would tell me when I might expect her. There was a situation ! I had told her I thought she would do well in New York, but I could not know. How I despised then that conversational mode of learning French. I wrote her at once that perhaps I had been extravagant in my praises of my native land—that I did not know enough about painting to be *sure* of her success—that in our conversations the wish had been the father of the thought, etc., etc. But she never received that letter. Before it reached the other side she had started. She had written me again about when to expect her. Then I set about making inquiries and preparations. On all sides they said, " If she is a good artist she will succeed ; it all depends on that. She can be profitably employed either in teaching or in painting pictures, if she is really competent.'' As I did not know whether she answered that description or not I was naturally anxious, but the next thing was to get a pleasant home for her. We were still at the boarding-house where my family had stayed during my absence. It was, however, full, much to our regret, for my wife was now deeply interested in the success of my new *protegée*. However, I found a very pleasant place for her near by, and not knowing what condition her finances would be in at first, assumed all necessary responsibility.

In due time I received a note from a little French hotel in Murray street : " I have arrived ; please come for me." I went at once, and found her none the worse for her voyage. I took her first to see my wife. The two had heard much of each other, but as one could speak no English and the other no French, their meeting was exceedingly amusing. They smiled sweetly on each other, and said all sorts of pleasant and complimentary things, which I interpreted to the best of my ability. I believe my wife did manage to say " thank you " in French for some gloves that Mademoiselle had brought her. Then we all went to the boarding-place that had been arranged for her. She was much pleased with it, and the landlady was evidently much prepossessed in favor of her new lodger. Next we went to the Spingler Institute, where I introduced her to the French teacher, who was a French lady, and to Mr. and Mrs. Abbott. In a day or two she was introduced to the wife of one of the most distinguished physicians of New York, a Swiss lady from one of the French-speaking cantons, and by her to some other important people of the city. Everybody was delighted with her grace and beauty, and she *was* a good artist. Some pictures that she brought with her were exhibited in Williams & Stevens' window (they were the great picture-sellers of New York then), and were much admired. She began by teaching and painting some portraits, and in a very short time was fully occupied. It proved that she brought some money with her, but she would not have needed any assistance if she had not, for she was soon in receipt of a much larger income than she had ever enjoyed in France. She sent for her sister in a few weeks, but the younger lady, who was still in delicate health, found our climate so uncongenial that she soon returned to France.

And now for the *dénouement*. The second year after Miss Adèle's arrival a rich Fifth avenue family, with whom she was a great favorite, invited her to spend the summer with them at the White Mountains. There a wealthy gentleman from Cuba fell in love with her, and in the autumn they were married. A year afterward I received a letter from her, filled with praises of her beautiful boy, and calling down blessings upon my head as the cause, to some extent, of her happiness. So the conversational mode of improving in French did not turn out so badly after all. At all events, it was permitted that the promises I made in so careless and unthinking a fashion should all be fulfilled.

And now to return to Paris. After the first of May, 1851, the Americans that came from London were in a state of great mortification and disgust at the United States exhibit in the great Crystal Palace Exposition—the first affair of the kind in which all nations united. They said that the United States Commissioners had insisted upon a large space, and that it was not half filled, and that the chief things there were some plows, and a barrel of shoe-pegs. That was extravagant, of course, but the American department did look plain and uninviting in comparison with the elegant profusion of things from the older and nearer nations; but more of that later.

Soon after the fourth of July one of my American friends and I started for London *en route* for home. This gentleman was Levi P. Homer, a young Bostonian, who had been studying music abroad for a year or two, and had been with us at Madame Maffit's for a few weeks. He was afterward Professor of Music in Harvard College, and was, I think, the immediate predecessor of the present occupant of that office. He died many years ago. We left Paris on a Friday morning, and arrived in London that afternoon. The first thing that attracted my attention there was an announcement of the " Messiah " at Exeter Hall. It was to be given that evening. My friend was too much shaken up by that abomination of all travelers—the passage across the channel —to go, and I was scarcely better, but I could not miss that opportunity. It was a magnificent performance—six hundred in the chorus, a large orchestra and organ, Clara Novello, Miss Dolby, Sims Reeves and Carl Formes (at his best) taking the solos, and all under the direction of Sir Michael Costa. The oratorio was not " cut," and took four hours in performance. The alto was sung mostly by men, and one reason of the great perfection of the chorus work was that a large proportion of the singers on all the parts knew the music by heart, and could keep their eyes upon the conductor.

An incident illustrating the loyalty of the English people to their old favorites comes freshly to my mind in connection with that concert. I was early, and found myself seated by a stout, plainly dressed man, who, with myself, was evidently much interested in seeing the audience gather. After a while the members of the orchestra began to take their places, and when an old man with a violoncello entered, the audience applauded, my neighbor joining heartily. The old man bowed and quietly took his seat. I said: "What is that applause for?" "Oh, that's Mr. Lindley," responded my neighbor, with a strong Yorkshire accent; "he used to be a great solo player, and we always give him a hand in remembrance of old times." I remembered then to have heard that name as the famous 'cellist of the previous generation. This led to further conversation with the good-natured Yorkshireman, who was much interested to learn that I was an American. He introduced a young lady who was sitting by his side by saying: "My daughter and I always come up to London when they sing the 'Messiah.'" A week from that night the same company precisely gave "Elijah." The value of those two performances to me in after years was very great. They were authentic and authoritative, both for tempos and style. Of the "Messiah" the tradition was in a direct line from its great author, and "Elijah" had been conducted by Mendelssohn himself but a few years before in Birmingham.

The day after we arrived in London we went to the Crystal Palace, the same magnificent building that is now in Sydenham. It was then in Hyde Park. As we approached we noticed an odd-looking machine on one side of the entrance, evidently not thought worthy a place inside. The papers made a good deal of fun of it, as they had of several other "Yankee notions," not realizing what a commotion that weather-beaten apparatus would make when the time for test and trial came. It was a McCormick Reaper.

When I entered the United States Department I went up to a short, thick-set man, with a most jovial and contented expression of countenance, who was sitting on a high box, swinging his feet in true Yankee fashion. "Why, Hobbs, what are you doing here?" was my first greeting. I had not seen him since the old Musical Education Society days in Boston, where he was one of my cronies on the base. He was a machinist by trade, and I knew him then as a bright, pushing fellow. "Oh, I'm representing the Day & Newell lock." "Well, how are you getting along?" "First-rate; look in the papers to-morrow and you'll see." I told him I had but just come, and did not know what was going on. Would he tell me all about it? "Well, the Bramah lock has been the great lock of England for a long time. It is on the vaults and safes of the Bank of England, and is used everywhere here as the best. There has been a safe in the window of its sales-room for years with this legend upon it: 'There are twenty pounds within this safe which will be given to any one who can pick this lock.'" "And are you going to do it?" "Yes; I have been to see it to-day, and have told them that I should open it to-morrow." "And are you sure you can do it?" "Yes; I don't like the idea of picking a lock, but that is the best way to introduce mine, and, besides, that twenty pounds will come in handy." And he did it. It took him just as many minutes as there were pounds that went into his pocket, and it made a great sale for his lock. I think it was subsequently used in the bank and other public places.

The first sewing machine was there in charge of two brothers who had been members of Park Street choir. A Philadelphia chairmaker had a new reclining chair that could be adjusted in many ways. Prince Albert, who was the projector of the great enterprise, and Queen Victoria, used often to go in and look about early in the day, before the public was admitted. The Prince was especially interested in everything that saved labor, or that made in any way for the welfare of the people. One day this Philadelphian, who, by the way, was originally from Vermont, was in great spirits. He said: "I've had the Queen in that chair this mornin'. I put her into all the positions I could

think of, and the Prince he laughed well, and now I'm goin'
to put a sign up: ' The Queen has set in that chair, and anybody else who wants to set in it has got to pay a shillin'.' "
We left our enterprising countryman anticipating great results from his scheme.

Of the general and costly magnificence of the Exposition
it is not worth while to speak, for the world is familiar with
such things now. One thing, however, that was there has
not been seen in any other country, and that was the " Kohi-
noor," the enormous diamond belonging to the British crown
jewels. In this case it was the real article, and not the paste
substitute which has sometimes been shown. It was in an
octagonal glass and iron case, on an iron pedestal, and was
surrounded by a strong railing that prevented people from
getting within two or three feet of it, and to further protect
it was guarded day and night by four soldiers.

When the time came for examining the exhibits and
awarding the prizes a great change took place in the public
mind in regard to the American Department. The rusty,
weather-beaten machine, that had been the butt of so many
jokes at the expense of the Yankees, was taken out onto a
smooth English grain field and set going. The effect was
magical. Could this be the ungainly thing they had laughed
at? Such reaping had not been dreamed of. The Englishman loves fair play, and we got full credit for that, and many
other things that had not seemed to be of much account
until they were put to use. To crown all, about the same
time the new yacht "America" beat the English yacht
squadron in a race off the Isle of Wight. The Americans
held up their heads after that, and were a little ashamed
that they had distrusted the ability of Uncle Sam to hold
his own in this contest of nations.

We stayed in London about four weeks, and then went
to Southampton, where the Havre steamers touched, and

took the Humboldt for home. It was a remarkably smooth voyage, though one incident as we neared our coast I shall never forget. I was a little seasick all the way—just enough to be nervous and apprehensive, especially after hearing stories of running into icebergs or fishing craft, and the marvelous things about the density of the fog banks off Newfoundland. But one night I went to bed quite peaceful, for the moon was bright and the air clear, and the ocean almost as calm as a mill-pond. About midnight, however, I was awakened by sudden orders and hurried footsteps overhead, and felt immediately that the ship's side had hit against something, for she heeled over in a most perceptible and alarming way. I sprang out of my berth and called to Mr. Homer, who occupied the upper one, that the ship had struck something. I thought of fishing smacks and icebergs, and was in a state of great nervous excitement while trying to get into my clothes. I feared every moment that something worse would happen. My friend started to get out of his berth, but, being but half awake, lost his balance and came down on my back as I was stooping over to put on my shoes. I thought the ship had gone to the bottom. I believe I was never so frightened before, or have ever been since. As soon as I recovered I rushed upon deck, and found we were within a hundred yards of the rocks of Cape Race, the eastern point of Newfoundland. Strange as it may seem, the officers of the ship had made a mistake in their reckoning, and did not suppose they were within a hundred miles of the cape. They took the wall before them for a fog bank, and if every man had not been at his post when they discovered their error, and had not obeyed the sudden orders instantly, we should have crashed straight on to the rocks and gone down like a broken egg-shell. We afterward learned that our captain had been on the Havre packets (sailing vessels) many years, but that this was his first voyage on a steamer.   He said it was a receding wave that made the ship heel over, but she went into dry-dock when we arrived in New York, and was there some weeks, so we knew she was hit.

It was a hot August morning when we landed, and I remember thinking that everybody we met on Broadway looked sick—they were so pale and thin.   The contrast to the ruddy English people we had just left was striking. New Yorkers and the American people generally are healthier looking now than they were in those days.   The women wear thicker shoes and take more exercise, and both men and women know better about eating, drinking, and the laws of health generally.

CHAPTER VIII.

1851–1853, NEW YORK—"THE FLOWER QUEEN" AND THE FIRST
"ROSE"—"WURZEL" AND "THE HAZEL DELL"—MY BEST
PIANO PUPIL—THE FIRST NORMAL MUSICAL INSTITUTE—
"DANIEL" AND EARLY BOOKS—THE NEW HOUSE AT WIL-
LOW FARM, AND THE SINGING IN THE VILLAGE CHURCH
—MY FIRST MUSICAL CONVENTION—THE VALUE OF A
SPECIALTY—THE OLD VIOLIN—EARLY ORCHESTRAS.

I FOUND my family at the old home in North Reading.
We had a week or so more of vacation, and then I went
back to New York and resumed my work. The first need
I felt was for something new for my classes, especially at
Rutgers and Spingler Institutes, to sing. This was in the
autumn of 1851. Mr. Bradbury had given some floral concerts with children at the Broadway Tabernacle, and at a
recent one had introduced some selections in a connected
series. This gave me the idea that a little musical play
might be made for girls and young ladies that would be useful. I cast about for a subject. It was not difficult to find
one; the whole world was open to me, for nothing of the
kind had been done. I soon decided that the subject should
be flowers choosing a queen, and that the little play should
be called "The Flower Queen."

At the Institution for the Blind there was at that time a
lady who had been a pupil there, but was now a teacher,
who had a great gift for rhyming, and, better still, had a
delicate and poetic imagination. The name of Fanny Crosby was not known then beyond the small circle of her personal friends, but it is now familiar, especially wherever

Gospel songs are sung. I used to tell her one day in prose what I wanted the flowers or the Recluse to say, and the next day the poem would be ready—sometimes two or three of them. I generally hummed enough of a melody to give her an idea of the meter and rhythmic swing wanted, and sometimes played to her the entire music of a number before she undertook her work. It was all the same. Like many blind people her memory was great, and she easily retained all I told her. After receiving her poems, which rarely needed any modification, I thought out the music, perhaps while going from one lesson to another, (the distances were so great that I had to spend a good deal of time every day in omnibuses or street cars,) and then I caught the first moment of freedom to write it out. Sometimes this was a half hour before dinner or supper, sometimes a little while between lessons, and sometimes an hour at night. This went on until the cantata was finished.

I can truly say that I had no other thought in this work than my own needs. I did not know that it would ever be heard outside of the walls of the institutions in which I was teaching. I had to have it printed because I needed so many copies myself, and this time it fell into good hands. The two older sons of Dr. Mason were then book-sellers and publishers in New York, under the firm name of Mason Brothers. They willingly undertook to supply me with copies, and they said, "We'll publish it regularly—others may want what you want," and so it proved.

I have often been glad that I did not begin earlier to write for publication. It was not a noble motive that restrained me, but our foolishness is often overruled to our advantage. By delaying I had become better equipped. I had heard a good deal of good music, and had been obliged to teach some of a high order. Everything that my blind pupils sang I had to know in the most thorough manner.

My acquaintance with some of the best musicians of the day was such as to bring me into close contact with what they performed and liked, and in my family we were familiar with music of a grade considerably above that of the popular music of the day. The reservoir was, therefore, much better filled than it would have been if I had commenced when urged to do so by the friends of whom I have spoken, and the comparatively simple music that I have written from that time to this has included a greater variety of subjects, and has been better in quality in consequence.

I saw at once that mine must be the "people's song," still, I am ashamed to say, I shared the feeling that was around me in regard to that grade of music. When Stephen C. Foster's wonderful melodies (as I now see them) began to appear, and the famous Christy's Minstrels began to make them known, I "took a hand in" and wrote a few, but put "G. Friederich Wurzel" (the German for Root) to them instead of my own name. "Hazel Dell" and "Rosalie, the Prairie Flower" were the best known of those so written. It was not until I imbibed more of Dr. Mason's spirit, and went more among the people of the country, that I saw these things in a truer light, and respected myself, and was thankful when I could write something that all the people would sing.

"The Flower Queen" served an excellent purpose, both as an incentive to work on the part of the classes, and as an entertainment for the friends of the schools. I served in the double capacity of Recluse and stage manager in the first performances, and fear the latter character appeared sometimes during the performance of the former much to the detriment of that dignitary. However, we always rehearsed thoroughly, and the success of those first representations was all that could be desired. The first "Rose" is worth telling about.

Two or three years before, I noticed one day a strange voice among my four hundred at Rutgers. It did not seem loud, but it pervaded the whole room and was exceedingly rich in quality. It seemed so mature that I looked among the young ladies for it at first, but there was no stranger among them. Then I stepped down from the platform and walked back among the younger girls and soon discovered her, a small brunette, twelve or thirteen years old, with laughing eyes and a profusion of dark, wavy hair hanging unconfined about a handsome, dark face. That was her first day at the school, but she soon became our *prima donna*, and the name of Annie Thomas will not soon be forgotten by those who heard her during those years at Rutgers, and afterward in her more prominent musical life in New York.

I used to take my pupils occasionally to hear the blind people sing. Annie was a great favorite there. She not only captivated the class, but in a special and particular way a young gentleman who not only could hear her voice, but see her face. He was a theological student, temporarily teaching there. He had a younger brother who was a part of the time in the Institution, I think, as an office boy. This theological student sought an introduction to my young lady and I introduced him. A few years after he married her. He is now the Rev. Wm. Cleveland, of Forestport, N. Y., and the office boy was, not long ago, President of the United States.

Speaking of my best singer in New York, on account of her connection with a well-known personage, brings to my mind my best piano pupil, a lovely young girl of thirteen or fourteen. If you will read Charles Dudley Warner's "My Summer in a Garden," you will be much amused at his allusions to his wife who was this young girl. I hope she has not forgotten the Cramer's studies she played so well.

With every Teacher's Class and Convention that I at-

tended with Mr. Mason and Mr. Webb I became more interested in the improvement of the teachers who came to be
instructed. I saw how inadequate the time was for much
improvement, not only in my department (the voice), but in
the art of teaching and in harmony and general musical
culture. Early in 1852 I conceived the idea of having a
three months' session for this work. It must be in the summer, because then the teachers had more leisure. It must
be in the city of New York, for I must be there where my
work was. I knew the expenses of advertising and place
of meeting would be large, but I believed that from all the
States and Canada enough teachers, and those who wished
to become such, would come, to save the enterprise from
pecuniary loss.

I went immediately to Boston, where Mr. Mason still
lived, and told him my plan. It did not strike him at first
as feasible. He did not believe any considerable number of
persons could be induced to come, especially from a distance,
on account of the great expense of traveling and of such a
stay in New York City, in addition to the cost of instruction.
I said, "Well, I am going to have such a class. You are the
proper person to appear at the head of it, and to be the real
head when it comes to the teaching, but I do not expect you
to do any of the work of getting it up; I'll see to that. It
will be a better opportunity than you have ever had to make
your ideas of notation, teaching, and church music really
known, for you will have time enough thoroughly to indoc-
trinate people with them, and that you know you never have
had in Teachers' Classes and Conventions."

I knew this would move him if anything would. No
word of money or remuneration for his services passed
between us, and I take this opportunity to say that Lowell
Mason was the most misjudged man in this respect that I
ever knew. He had plenty of money. It came in large

sums from his works, but I do not believe he ever made a plan to make money, unless when investing his surplus funds.   In his musical work it was always " Is this the best thing—will it be received—will it do the most good?" It was a clear case in its sphere of seeking first what was right and finding that all other things were added. And now that I am about it, I will say further of this remarkable man, that although great in every way, intellectually and morally as well as musically, he was like a child if any error could be pointed out in his works or defect in his teaching. It was not often that either thing happened, but when it did, it was " Is that so? Let us see," and prompt correction took place whenever he saw he was wrong. A favorite saying with him was, " Error makes us weak—truth makes us strong."

As I am writing these recollections I open my morning paper and the following item catches my eye. It is worth inserting here, but first I will explain that Mr. Mason was a Massachusetts man by birth, but lived for a while in Savannah, Ga. From there he was induced to return to Boston, by some prominent citizens who knew of his gifts, and believed that he could inaugurate the musical reform that they felt was needed.   " Missionary Hymn " was, I am quite sure, his first publication.

When Bishop Heber's famous missionary hymn, " From Green-land's Icy Mountains," which he wrote in 1824 when in Ceylon, first reached this country, a lady in Savannah was much impressed with the beauty of it, and was particularly anxious to find a tune suited to it. She ransacked her music in vain, and then chancing to remember that in a bank down the street was a young clerk who had consider-able reputation as a musical genius, she decided to ask him to write a tune to fit it. He readily complied with her request, and the mel-ody thus dashed off is to-day sung all over the world, and is insepar-ably connected with the hymn. The young bank clerk was Lowell Mason.

Mr. Mason finally agreed to be at the head of the enterprise, which I decided to call "The Normal Musical Institute," but he said he had promised to go to England for a short visit. "When did I wish to commence?" "In June," I told him—June, July and August, I thought, should be the months. Well, he would be back in time without doubt. Then I went back to New York, and with Mason Brothers, the publishers, I took a different line of argument. I said: "It will be a great thing for the sale of your father's books to have his methods and music better understood than they can be in the shorter gatherings. (I had no books of my own then for such work.) Will you do the work of making the right people know of this all over the country?" They said they would, and they did. The responses were most encouraging, but a change took place in our plans. A few weeks before the time set to begin, Mr. Mason wrote that he could not be back until in the summer, perhaps not until the autumn. He had found work to do in England that delighted him, and that he felt was useful, and we must go on with the Institute without him, or defer the opening until the next summer. The brothers said, "We believe this is going to be a success, and if you will put it off we will not only pay all the expenses incurred thus far, but all the expenses of advertising it for next year. To this I readily agreed, as I did not wish to begin without the "master." So the notice of postponement, with explanations, was sent wherever the Institute had been advertised, and to all who wrote about coming, and the matter rested.

It will be of interest to mention that Mr. Mason's work in England had reference principally to congregational singing, although he gave some lessons in his incomparable way in the elementary principles of music. The Rev. John Curwen, father of the present Messrs. Curwen, and founder of the tonic-sol-fa method of notation, was present at many of Mr. Mason's lectures and lessons, and was greatly interested

in both. Tonic-sol-fa was in its infancy then. Mr. Mason
spoke of it as a simple notation for the poor people of Mr.
Curwen's congregation. He had no idea that its use would
extend much farther than that. It is certain that these two
men—the one having exercised a vast influence for good on
the singing of the people in America, and the other destined
to perform a similar use in England—were sincerely attached
to each other.

In the summer of 1853 the first Normal Musical Institute
was held. Its sessions were in Dodworth's Hall, Broadway,
New York, and continued three months. The principal
teachers were Lowell Mason, Thomas Hastings, Wm. B.
Bradbury and myself; assistant teachers, John Zundel,
J. C. Woodman, and some others, for private lessons, whose
names I do not now recall. The terms were $25 for the
normal course; $50 if private lessons were added. There
were upwards of a hundred from abroad, and enough singers from the city to make a good chorus. I think we met
but one evening a week for chorus practice; certainly not
more than two. Working as we did all through the day in
the hot city, we did not think it safe to add much evening
work. We gave no concerts. It was years before the
"Normal" thought of deriving any revenue in that way.
In fact, it was not exactly business to any of us (excepting
to those who gave private lessons). Each had his regular
occupation in other ways. As the years went on, modifications in many things were made, and improvements in some
of the studies introduced, but the main objects of the institution and the program of daily work have remained in this,
and have been adopted in the other institutes that have
sprung up since, essentially as in that first memorable
session.

About this time I gathered the best of the material together that we had been using in Rutgers and Spingler

Institutes, and with some new music, and an elementary course taken from Mr. Mason's books, embodied all in the "Academy Vocalist," my first work of any pretension for schools. Through the energy of the publishers, and the fact that other teachers and schools experienced the same needs that we felt, the book had considerable success. The "Flower Queen" quickly became popular, and "Hazel Dell" began the run which was not to end until the boys whistled it and the hand organs played it from Maine to Georgia, and no ambition for a song-writer could go higher than that.

These successes gave me a new inclination to write, and I decided that I would next make a cantata for my choir. At this time one of the students in the Union Theological Seminary was C. M. Cady, who, afterward, with my brother E. T. Root, started the firm of Root & Cady in Chicago. I decided on "Daniel" as the subject, and Mr. Cady and Fanny Crosby helped me in preparing the words. About the time the cantata was completed I was approached with reference to making a church-music book with Mr. Bradbury. This I was very glad to do, and "The Shawm" was the result. All interested thought it would be a good plan to print the new cantata at the end of the book—that many of its choruses could be used as anthems, and that some of its solos and quartets might also find a place in church service. So that was done; but in order that Mr. Bradbury's name might rightfully appear as joint author, I took out two of my numbers from the cantata, and he filled their places. "The Shawm" was a success, but the cantata was so much called for, separate from the book, that it was not bound up with it after the first or second edition. Its place was filled with set pieces, and "Daniel" has been printed as a book by itself ever since.

And now I decided to build a new house on the old place at North Reading, not only better to accommodate the clan which assembled there every summer, but for the greater comfort of the dear people who stayed there all the time. So one of my boy friends, then a prosperous carpenter in the town, came to New York, and we agreed upon a plan which on his return met the approval of the home folks and was speedily carried out. The delight with which we went into the new and completed house at Willow Farm at our next vacation can not be described. No palace ever gave kingly occupants greater pleasure. In the old red house the swaying branches of the great elm did not reach our windows; now we were right up under them. There, close by, at the end of a long, graceful bough, was where the oriole, in his gorgeous red costume, swung his hammock every year, and there it was, as we looked, rocking as of yore in the summer breeze.

It was not only delightful for us to be at the old home in the summer, but a great gratification to give some extra pleasure to the old friends of the little town. This was principally done by singing in church on Sunday, though we sometimes gave a concert on a week evening, to which everybody was invited. There were so many of us, and always some musical friends to swell the number, that we had an excellent choir—one that would have been acceptable anywhere. We all remember well a tall, shy boy, who then was an apprentice to a farmer in the town, who used to listen with wonder and delight to our music, and who has told me since that he could not have looked upon princes with greater awe than he did upon us in those days. He is now one of Chicago's millionaires. One of his "deals" on the Board of Trade will ever be memorable in the history of that institution. Six hundred and fifty thousand dollars clear in one day, not to mention the enormous profits of other days during the operation! His name is B. P. Hutchinson. A few years ago we rode up from Boston one summer day, to see the old friends. He enjoyed greatly being where people called him " Ben," and treated him as if he were no more than common folks.

My life now went on very pleasantly in New York, but I began to be asked to conduct musical conventions in the neighboring states. My connection with the Teachers' Classes, and the " Normal" recently held, and with Mr. Bradbury in " The Shawm," had brought me more before the singers of the country. I declined at first, partly because I did not like to take the responsibility of the entire conduct of one of those gatherings, and partly because I did not care to break into my regular work. But finally I decided to try it, and accepted a call from Sussex county, New Jersey, and now I miss again my lost diary. With that I could have told exactly when and where I had my first convention experience; who employed me; who the clergymen and prominent musical people of the section were; where I stayed, and who invited me to dinner or tea; who were the solo singers; what books I used, and how much I received. But as it is I can only recall a pleasant scene in a hilly country, with a crowd of happy people, who took kindly to my way of teaching and entertaining them.

My first successful song ("Hazel Dell") was published in 1852 by Wm. Hall & Son, who then occupied a store on the corner of Broadway and Park Place. This was followed by a contract with this house, by which I was to give them all my sheet music publications for three years. My brother had returned from the South, and becoming tired, as he said, of being, as a teacher, only "Mr. Root's brother," decided to learn the music business, and was then a clerk in the Hall establishment.

The Messrs. Hall were the publisher's of Gottschalk's and Wm. Vincent Wallace's music at that time, and I frequently met those gentlemen there. Wallace, who may be remembered as the author of "Maritana," an opera quite popular at one time, and still somewhat sung, and of many fine songs and pianoforte compositions, was a distinguished pianist and a fine violinist. As a concert player upon *either* instrument he would have been a success, but undertaking to give concerts upon *both*, he failed. It is a curious fact that the public will not give a musician a high place in its esteem if he makes himself prominent in two or more specialties, however excellent he may be in them.

I remember once seeing a great conductor step down from his platform and play a solo upon the violin. It was done, of course, extremely well, but everybody felt that he had "stepped down" in more senses than one. Carl Zerrahn, the able and popular conductor of the Handel and Haydn Society of Boston, and of the Worcester and other Festivals, came over to this country with the Germania orchestra as a solo flute player, but I dare say that not a dozen people of the tens of thousands who have placed him, in their estimation, upon the highest round of the ladder in his specialty, know that he plays that instrument at all, and were he to take his flute some day instead of his baton, and give them a solo, he might astonish them, but he would have to pay for that pleasure by "stepping down" a round, musically, in their estimation. Mr. Zerrahn sings well, but he never sings a song. He understands perfectly the value of having but one specialty in the public mind.

"Hall's" was a famous rendezvous for musical people. A frequent visitor was Captain Brooks, who owned and ran a little steamboat from New York to Bridgeport, Conn. He was an enthusiastic and indefatigable collector of old violins. He would often rush in and want some one to go down to his boat with him and see a new violin—"a real Stradivarius" or "Guarnarius," or something of the kind. He could not play much, but through his great interest in the subject he had become a pretty good judge of the instrument, and if he was sometimes deceived as to the maker he had no poor ones in his collection. One day he was particularly excited, and wanted some of us to go with him and see a violin that he had just paid some hundreds of dollars for. A slight, smooth-faced, decidedly handsome young fellow, who was known to play the violin well, was there, and Captain Brooks induced him to go and try it. I could see that the young violinist was skeptical as to the great merits of the instrument, as claimed by the excited Captain. But when he took it into his hand, before he touched bow to string, his whole manner changed (though what he could see in that glance I could not imagine), and when he tucked it lovingly under his chin the rest of the world was nothing to him for half an hour or more. He was entranced, and so were we. It was a rare and beautiful instrument, and the young player was Theodore Thomas.

Speaking of the "Germania" reminds me of the delight with which we listened to the first fine orchestra that came to this country. It was called the Steyermarkische orchestra. It was not large, about twenty players, if I remember rightly, but they played *in tune*, and the smoothness so produced was a revelation. Their shading and pianissimo playing were also new and delightful. They had a successful tour and went home. This must have been about 1846. Then came the Germania orchestra, with Carl Bergmann for conductor. They gave concerts in our principal cities, and finally disbanded here, most of its members remaining on this side of the water.

The only other foreign orchestra to come to this country was Jullien's; I forget whether just before or just after the Germania, but probably at about the same time. Jullien was a talented man and an able conductor, but he was much laughed at for his flashy taste in dress and his funny affectations. He brought with him a gorgeous conductor's stand and platform, and a magnificent chair, all apparently of ebony and gold. After each number he would sink into this great chair and let his arms fall as if the splendid perform-ance had entirely exhausted him, for the performances, al-though of the sensational order, were fine. Bottesini, the great contra-bass player, was in this company. I see he is prominent in Europe now as an author and conductor.

But it was the oboe player who created the greatest sen-sation. He was the first one here to continue a tone while taking breath. I shall never forget the curious effect upon the audience when, at a cadenza, the accompaniment ceased and a long tone commenced. After it had continued to the utmost bounds of the longest breath there was a distressed holding of breath by the audience, and when it still went on, strong and clear, the excitement was intense. A little longer and everybody saw he must have taken breath somehow, and the relief and applause were tremendous. The instru-ment requires but little breath, and he could supply it from the mouth on the principle of a bellows, while filling his lungs through the nostrils.

We do not now have to get orchestras from the other side of the water, nor to go over there to hear the best. Theodore Thomas has rendered both unnecessary by the impulse he has given to the formation of first-class orches-tral combinations in this country.

CHAPTER IX.

1853–1855, NEW YORK—A FRANK STATEMENT—GENIUSES IN MUSIC—"THE SHINING SHORE"—EARLY BOOKS—THE FIRST AMERICAN-MADE DOCTOR OF MUSIC—EARLY CONVENTIONS AT RICHMOND, VA., AND IN THE WEST—PREPARING TO LEAVE NEW YORK—HOW THE NORMAL WENT TO NORTH READING.

BEFORE going on to speak more at length of my compositions and books, I desire to make a frank statement with regard to myself and my work in that line; and my first remark is, that I never felt in the least that I had a "call" to be a musical composer. My first efforts, as I have shown, were made to supply my own wants, and it was only on finding that they were in a good degree successful for myself and others that I continued them.

I can truly say I never dreamed of eminence as a writer of music, and never had fame for an object. Some of my friends who knew who "Wurzel" was, used to say: "Aim high; he who aims at the sun will reach farther than he will who has a lower object for a mark." But I saw so many failures on the part of those who were "aiming high" in the sense intended, and trying to do useless great things, that I had no temptation in that direction, but preferred to shoot at something I could hit.

I did, on two or three occasions, write what I knew would not be needed, but in every case had an object. Once, two prizes were offered by the publishers of a musical paper in New York—fifty dollars for the best four-part song, and twenty-five dollars for the second best. I sent in two, anon-

ymously, (as all had to do,) and took both prizes. Two of
the judges were loud despisers of " trash," as they indiscrimi-
nately called all simple music, and were much disgusted
when they learned who had taken the prizes.

Friends used to say: " Root, why don't you do something
better than ' Hazel Dell,' and things of that grade?" I used
to answer: " If you and other musicians wished to use songs
of a higher grade, either for teaching or for your own singing, do you suppose you would take mine when you could
get Schubert or Franz, or even Abt, at the same price or
less? " They were generally silent at that, and then I would
tell them that in the elementary stages of music there were
tens of thousands of people whose wants would not be supplied at all if there were in the world only such music as
they (the critics) would have; but

> " Convince a man against his will—
> He's of the same opinion still."

So they continued harping upon the well-worn subject. At
last I thought I would publish a song or two above the grade
of the " People's song." It was much easier to write where
the resources were greater; where I did not have to stop and
say, " That interval is too difficult," or " That chord won't
do," and I produced two or three that I knew would never
be wanted to any extent. But they gave me the opportunity,
when the old question came, " Why don't you do something
better?" to say " Have you ever seen or heard of ' Gently,
Ah, Gently,' or ' Pictures of Memory?' " To which they
would have to answer " No," and I could say " That is why
I do not write ' something better,' as you call it. Neither
you nor any one else would know anything about my work
on that grade, and I should be wasting my time in trying to
supply the wants of a few people, who are already abundantly
supplied by the best writers of Europe." Then they would
say, " Well, it is nothing to write those little songs." I re-

member one, especially, then an eminent musician in New York, who said: "I could write a dozen in a day," and, thinking there might be money in it, he did try under a *nom de plume*. But his dozen or less of "simple songs" slumbered quietly on the shelves of a credulous publisher until they went to the paper mill. It is easy to write correctly a simple song, but so to use the material of which such a song must be made that it will be received and live in the hearts of the people is quite another matter.

Geniuses among musical composers, that is, those who invent and give to the world new forms and harmonies *that live*, are rare—but two or three appear in a century. Of such, Beethoven in his day and Wagner in this, are conspicuous examples. Then there are great composers, who, although not inventors in the above sense, make use of existing material in such new and wonderful ways that their music not only delights and benefits the world, but is regarded in an important sense as original. Of such it seems to me that Mendelssohn is in the highest rank.

In all grades from the simplest to the highest—from Stephen C. Foster to Wagner, and in every kind of instrumental music, compositions divide themselves into two classes in another way. In one class are the comparatively few compositions having that mysterious vitality of which I have spoken; that power to retain their hold upon the hearts of the people after their companions of the same grade, and by the same composer perhaps, are forgotten. In the other class are those which create a temporary interest if any, and soon pass away. I do not think a composer ever knows when that mysterious life enters his work. If I may judge by my own experience, successes are usually surprises, and the work that we think best while we are doing it, is liable to be considered in a very different light by the public.

That applies, however, to single compositions and not to

books. One may think he is making a good instruction book, or putting together a good collection of music, without being mistaken. I should like to enlarge upon this point when I come to speak of particular compositions. All I want seen now is, that I am simply one, who, from such resources as he finds within himself, makes music for the people, having always a particular need in view. This, it seems to me, is a thing that a person may do with some success, without being either a genius or a great composer.

My next book, I think, was the " Musical Album." It was on the plan of the "Academy Vocalist," and followed that work when my classes wanted something new. I now wrote some every day, taking the intervals between lessons and occasionally an evening for that purpose. I also took a course of lessons during one of those winters from an excellent harmonist and teacher, a Frenchman by the name of Girac.

Mason Brothers published a musical monthly called *The Musical Review*, and at one time I undertook to supply music for each number. I remember once when the boy came for copy I had none ready, but looking into the drawer of my desk I found a piece that I had written some months before and thrown aside as not being of much account. I sent this for want of something better. It was "There's Music in the Air," and illustrates what I was saying a little while ago about not knowing when we do that which will touch the popular heart.

But it was at Willow Farm that I enjoyed my writing and book-making most. However we might be confined in New York by the summer Normal, we always had two or three weeks before the autumn work commenced at the old place, or, I might say now, the new place. With the dear mother about the house, and father attending to farm matters, with children or grand-children always around one or

the other, an atmosphere was there which was very favorable
to the work I was doing. One day, I remember, I was working at a set of graded part-songs for singing classes, and
mother, passing through the room, laid a slip from one of
her religious newspapers before me, saying: "George, I
think that would be good for music." I looked, and the
poem began, "My days are gliding swiftly by." A simple
melody sang itself along in my mind as I read, and I jotted
it down, and went on with my work. That was the origin
of "The Shining Shore."

Later, when I took up the melody to harmonize it, it
seemed so very simple and commonplace that I hesitated
about setting the other parts to it. But I finally decided
that it might be useful to somebody, and completed it, though
it was not printed until some months afterward. When, in
after years, this song was sung in all the churches and Sunday-schools of the land, and in every land and tongue where
our missionaries were at work, and so demonstrated that it
had in it that mysterious life of which I have spoken, I tried
to see why it should be so, but in vain. To the musician
there is not one reason in melody or harmony, scientifically
regarded, for such a fact. To him, hundreds of others now
forgotten were better. I say so much about this little song
because it is a particularly good illustration of the fact that
the simplest music may have vitality as well as that which
is higher, and that the composer knows no more about it in
one case than in the other.

The newspaper slip containing this hymn which my
mother handed me had no author's name attached. It was
some years before I learned that it was the Rev. David Nelson who wrote it, and it was but recently that the following
sketch of his life, taken from "Asa Turner and His Times,"
was sent to me:

David Nelson was born in East Tennessee in 1793; graduated
from Washington College in 1809. He at first studied medicine, but
afterward entered the ministry and preached in Tennessee and Ken-
tucky, and finally removed to Missouri. He was six feet and two
inches high, and had a voice of great power and melody, which he
used with great success, anticipating the singing evangelist of to-
day.

He opened a plantation in Missouri in true southern style, but
an address by Theodore D. Weld changed his sentiments and led
him to say, "I will live on roast potatoes and salt before I will hold
slaves." He became an advocate of colonization, and, in 1831, at the
close of a camp-meeting, read a notice calling people to meet to dis-
cuss the project. Disorder followed, and Dr. Nelson was driven from
his home by a body of armed men. After three days and nights of
wandering he came to the great river, and made known his condition to friends in Quincy, Illinois, on the opposite side—there, far
away.

Hiding in the bushes, with the Mississippi at the foot of the
bluff "gliding swiftly by," and "friends passing over" to and from
a free state—a safe landing on which he could "almost discover," he
wrote on the backs of letters the Christian psalm of life, "My days
are gliding swiftly by."

Two members of the Congregational Church in Quincy, at dusk
paddled a "dug-out" across the river and fished in the slough near
the western shore. Learning by signs just where Dr. Nelson was,
they let their boat float down toward the Missouri "strand." With
huge strides the fugitive evangelist came down, and the slavehold-
ing scouts were foiled.

Dr. Nelson, well-nigh starved, asked if they had brought him
anything to eat. "Something in the bag," replied one of the
brethren, rowing with all his might. The brave but famished man
brought up from the bag at the stern only dried codfish and
crackers. Laughing heartily he said, "Well, I'm dependent on
Yankees, and shall have to be a Yankee myself after this, and I may
as well begin on codfish and crackers."

The chivalry crossed the river and demanded that Dr. Nelson
should be given up, but were told that he was under the laws of
Illinois, and slaveholders could not have him.

Dr. Nelson was commissioned by the Home Missionary Society
in Illinois, and, in addition to his regular work, made powerful and
touching anti-slavery addresses. He died in October, 1844.

From 1853 to 1855 inclusive the Normal Musical Institute was held in New York city, but every year my convention work, and, consequently, my knowledge of what the singers throughout the country needed, and could do, increased, and every year it became more and more apparent that the city was not a good place for Normals, not only on account of the heat but the expense.   So, in 1855, I decided to give up my city work as soon as it could be brought about, and devote myself wholly to conventions, Normal and authorship.   Meanwhile Mr. Mason had come to like New York, and his sons, who had prospered greatly there, induced him to leave his Boston home and settle in the great city.   They had some picturesque and valuable acres on the mountain side, in Orange, New Jersey, and soon the three families built and occupied fine residences there.

One day, soon after Mr. Mason came to New York to live, I called on Dr. Ferris, with whom I had been connected for some years at Rutgers Institute, and who was now Chancellor of the New York University, and said to him, "Could your institution confer the degree of Doctor of Music?"   "Certainly."   "Well, I think that that title has never been conferred upon an American by an American institution.   S. Parkman Tuckerman, of Boston, is the only American Doctor of Music that I know of, and his degree is from an English university."   I then said, "you know of Lowell Mason, and what he has done for church music and musical instruction in schools and among the people of this country."   "Yes."   "Well, what would you think of having your University the first in America to confer the title of Doctor of Music, and that that distinction should fall upon America's greatest musical educator?"   He thought so well of it that it was promptly done.

I said nothing to Mr. Mason about it until it was accomplished.   When it was, and was announced in one of the morning papers, I took a copy and went to his house. He was in his library, and as I entered I saluted him with " Good morning, *Doctor* Mason," emphasizing the title. He looked up, evidently wondering a little that I should be making a cheap joke of that kind, but immediately resumed his usual manner, and said, "I want to show you a tune that I have just made for this hymn." He was very full of that tune. I forget now what it was, but I remember that I had considerable difficulty in getting the idea of the title fully into his mind. I mention this as illustrating the fact, well known to Dr. Mason's friends, that he never sought honors or distinctions any more than he did wealth. He gave himself wholly to his work, and if other things came they must come without any effort on his part.

Among the early normals was Wm. C. Van Meter, then a typical far-westerner, a preacher, exhorter, singing-master, and I don't know what else. Eloquent and magnetic as a speaker in his strange western way, he created a great interest in the class. He stopped at the Astor House the night he arrived, and said that when he got up in the morning and saw such crowds going down toward a church that he saw a little way off (Trinity) he thought there must be a revival there, and he reported that he did not wait for his breakfast, but hurried down to join in the exercises. It took him some time to realize that that was the ordinary flow of humanity at the "down town " hour.

Mr. Van Meter was great for engineering musical conventions. He made up his mind that my talents were being wasted in New York and the East, and that I must go to the South and West to be properly appreciated. So he prepared the way, to begin with, in Richmond, Va. Let Mr. Van Meter get an audience together and there was no resisting him. He could make people laugh or cry at will, and paint in more glowing colors whatever he described than any man I ever knew. He always induced a large number of people to attend conventions, but he made it particularly hard for the conductor to meet the expectations that he raised.

I went to Richmond first to conduct a convention of Mr. Van Meter's getting up, and then some months after to conduct some performances of "The Flower Queen." On this latter occasion my home was the hospitable mansion of the father of "Marion Harland." She was then a young lady, writing her second book, her first, "Alone," having been a great success, making her famous at a bound. The Rev. Dr. Terhune, whose wife she now is, then a young man, was also a guest in that charming home. At the close of "The Flower Queen" class I was presented with my first gold-headed cane. In after years I had good reason to believe the donors would have been glad to break it over the head of the man who wrote war songs for the northern army. I hope and think that feeling has now entirely passed away. On both sides we did what we thought was right.

Speaking of Richmond reminds me that I conducted two conventions in Washington, not far from that time, one alone, and one assisted by Mr. Bradbury. I mention them because the second one was in the Smithsonian Institute when Prof. Henry was at its head. It was an effort to secure a more general attendance than such gatherings usually have, and was located at Washington to be near the southern states. I remember well the hearty welcome that Prof. Henry gave us, and the kind interest he took in the exercises. Nothing in the nature of popular education appealed to him in vain. He was a man of whom the nation is justly proud.

Under Mr. Van Meter's management I conducted two conventions in Quincy, Ills., and held a sort of short Normal in Jacksonville. A part of the program of this manager seemed always to be a present for the conductor at the close of the session. A silver cup, or a cane, or something for the table, always appeared at the closing concert, and I used to get Mr. Van Meter to help me return thanks, which he always did in the most eloquent manner. This remarkable man worked afterward, for some years, in and for the Five Points Mission in New York, and was for a still greater number of years in evangelistic labors in Rome, Italy.

It was hard to leave the work and the friends in New York. The work had been pleasant and the friends most kind and generous. Not a year of the ten that I had been there did the "commencements" fail to bring some token of remembrance, often costly, always useful, from schools or church. The last, and most valuable, was a solid silver tea-service to my wife when we left Mercer Street Church. We have all these gifts now, excepting some volumes of rare old English music, one of the annual presents from Rutgers. They were in my working room at the store at the time of the great fire, and shared the fate of my diary. Thinking of the presents, a beautiful silver cup reminds me of a class I had in those days at the "Brick Church" in Orange, New Jersey. I mention it because I think it will interest some of the many hundreds who now go daily to New York from there, to know that then three persons constituted the daily quota from that station.

As soon as I decided to leave New York I said to my old friends in North Reading, "If you will prepare a suitable place for us, I will have the Normal Musical Institute here next summer." They called a town meeting, at which was explained that the school would probably bring a hundred strangers there for three months, which would mean to the town some money and a good deal of music. Both ideas were well received and prompt action was taken. The building that was prepared for us is worth telling about.

When I was a boy there stood in the center of the village one of the old colonial "meeting houses." Its pews were square, its pulpit twelve or more feet high, with a "sounding board," like a huge bell, hanging above it, under which the minister stood. When at last the old building became too dilapidated for further use it was decided to tear it down and replace it with a modern structure. In the olden times all had worshiped there together with no dissensions, but, gradually, differences of opinion had arisen, and had been maintained as usual in such cases with a good deal of rancor. The "orthodox," as they were called, although not the most numerous, had the most money, and were the most willing to spend it for church purposes, so they had minister and service pretty much their own way. This did not tend to conciliate the other side, among whom were quite a number of Universalists, and who, in consequence, did not go much to "meeting."

Still they went on and put up the new building, nominally all together as a society, but it was really by the energy, and mostly by the money, of the first named party that it was accomplished. When the new edifice was completed, and a minister settled, the Universalists asked permission to have service there occasionally on Sunday afternoons. I don't think it was bigotry, so much as conscience, that led the orthodox party to refuse this request, but it was refused. Then the opposing elements got together and said, "This building belongs to the society, and a majority of the society can say what kind of preaching shall be in it." They probably would not have ignored the fact that they did very little toward building it if they had been kindly treated, but, as it was, they called a meeting of the society and managed to have a majority there to vote that a Universalist minister should occupy the new pulpit all the time.

I was but a boy then, but I remember how sad my old grandfather, one of the deacons of the church, looked the next day. However, he went immediately to work to get the names of those who would form a new society, specifically "orthodox," and build a new church. This was speedily done, but, as was foreseen, the Universalists, and those who sympathized with them but did not care much about "going to meeting," could not, or would not support a minister, and carry on Sunday services. So, in a short time, all such efforts were abandoned, and the building was useless for years, excepting as it was wanted for an occasional public gathering.

When, therefore, my proposition came, all differences ceased. Music and some general advantage to the town were grounds for a general amnesty, and it was voted unanimously to give up the building to the town, and then the town voted to prepare it for our use. This they found would make it just what was wanted for a convenient town hall.

CHAPTER X.

1856–1859, NORTH READING, MASS. — A GREAT SCHOOL IN A
SMALL TOWN—A VISIT FROM HENRY WARD BEECHER AND
MRS. STOWE — NATHAN RICHARDSON AND " ROSALIE, THE
PRAIRIE FLOWER "— WRITING AT WILLOW FARM — THE
" HAYMAKERS "— THE BEGINNING OF EAR TRAINING IN
CLASSES FOR HARMONY—" EXCEPT YE BECOME AS LITTLE
CHILDREN "—DISTINGUISHED VISITORS—RELATIVE PROFITS
OF CANTATA MAKER AND CANTATA GIVER—COMPOSITIONS
AS PROPERTY.

THE Normal Musical Institute commenced in North
Reading in 1856. The faculty then was Dr. Mason,
Mr. Webb, Mr. Bradbury and myself—August Kreissman,
of Boston, assisting in private lessons. The attendance was
large, and the difference between the city and this dear old
place delightful. As may readily be seen, so long as this
was the only institution of the kind in the country it not
only attracted people from afar, but it brought the prominent ones—those who at home were the principal teachers
or singers of their sections. All liked North Reading—the
place, the people and the arrangements for work. It *is* a
picturesque old town. Few views are more beautiful than
that which is seen from a hill near the village, of the Ipswich
River, there a small stream, winding in and out among the
trees that fringe its sides, far away in the meadows below;
and the walk over this hill and through the woods beyond
to Willow Farm was a great delight, especially to the western contingent, to whom the "rocks and rills and wooded
hills" of New England were a novelty.

The people of the town were always ready to do anything in their power to further the interests of the school and to make the stay of the strangers pleasant. The building, as it had been prepared for us, was very comfortable and convenient. Up one flight of stairs was the room where all assembled for the opening exercises, and where Dr. Mason's and other lessons to the whole Institute were given. On the ground floor was a larger hall, and below that a light basement. An additional room in a neighboring building was also used for some of the smaller classes. We had one evening rehearsal in the week in the hall, and one evening when the friends and neighbors could come and hear us sing.

It was a strange thing to hear such a chorus under such conductors as Dr. Mason and Mr. Webb in so small a place as our little village, but we never lacked an audience. Indeed, as the Normal did not then seek to derive any revenue from public performances, it was not long before we were troubled for room on our public evenings. We invited the neighbors, but we did not limit the neighborhood, and that gradually extended until it took in the neighboring towns, which were Andover on the north, Middleton and Lynnfield on the east, the other two Readings on the south, and Wilmington on the west. Every pleasant Friday, at five or six o'clock in the afternoon, vehicles of all sorts could be seen coming from one or more of these places to be in time for the evening sing. Those were happy times. How Dr. Mason's grand chorus work and the exquisite glee singing under Mr. Webb did ring and float out at the open windows of our pleasant hall, and away upon the summer air! Almost incredible stories were told of the distance at which our music was heard when the evenings were still.

One of the most prominent members of the Institute at North Reading was W. W. Killip, of Geneseo, N. Y. He was a man of excellent abilities, musical and otherwise, and he had a hearty, whole-souled way of meeting people that was very attractive. Mrs. Harriet Beecher Stowe then lived at Andover, near the Theological Seminary, seven miles from our town. Henry Ward Beecher generally spent a week or two with his sister there in the summer. The boys, or, I should say, all the members of the Institute, wanted to see Mr. Beecher, and Dr. Mason and I intended to ask him to spend a day with us, but Mr. Killip wouldn't wait. He said: "I'm not going to have any uncertainty about this; I'm going to see him and get him to set a day to come soon." Ordinarily, such a messenger, going on his own account, would not have fared so well as a simple bearer of an invitation from Dr. Mason, whom Mr. Beecher highly esteemed; but I knew Mr. Beecher, and was sure Mr. Killip's bluff, hearty way would interest him. He went, and came back triumphant. "Yes, he's coming next Tuesday." "Did he consent readily?" I asked. "He hesitated some," Mr. K. replied, "but I told him I'd vote for his candidate for Governor if he would come, and that settled it."

Not only Mr. Beecher, but Mrs. Stowe and the old father, Dr. Lyman Beecher, and Mr. Charles Beecher came. After the opening exercises and Dr. Mason's inimitable teaching lesson, the great desire of the class to hear Mr. Beecher speak was gratified. His beginning was most characteristic. He said: "I like the way your seats are arranged to bring the class near the platform and into close connection with the teacher, and your platform is just the right height. The devil always looks on when they are building a church to see how far they get the pews from the minister." Then Mr. Beecher, supposing a case, paced slowly the long way of the platform, to represent the wide space that was being left between minister and people, counting his steps in a crescendo of satisfaction, and bringing his fist down into his open palm at the close—all to represent what his satanic majesty would do and say under the circumstances: "One, two, three, four, five, six, seven; good! he'll never hit 'em!" Then he talked for half an hour on the relations of music to the church and the home, as only Mr. Beecher could talk. The whole party dined at Willow Farm and attended the afternoon chorus and glee singing, which they greatly enjoyed.

About the time that I began to be known as a successful song-writer Nathan Richardson (afterward author of "The Popular Piano Instructor") started a music publishing house in Boston. He had lived some years in Germany, and had come home filled with a strong desire to improve the musical tastes of the benighted people of his native land. This sounds like laughing at my old friend. Well, it is so; but not so much as I have done to his face many a time. The saying of the boatswain in "Pinafore" of the Admiral would have applied exactly here: "He means well, but he don't know." As it was, he determined that he would publish nothing but high-class music. I doubt if there was an American then whose compositions he would have taken as a gift. He had an elegant store on Washington street, fitted and furnished in an expensive manner through the generosity of an older brother, who had plenty of money, and who seemed delighted to aid Nathan in his praiseworthy efforts for the fatherland.

All went well for a few months. Musicians met there and greatly enjoyed a chat amid the luxurious surroundings, and they occasionally bought a piece of music when they found what their pupils could use. Some of the comparatively few amateurs of the city, who were advanced, also patronized the establishment, but it did not pay. At length both Nathan and the rich brother became convinced that they could not make people buy music, however fine, that they could not understand nor perform, and they found that calling the music that the common people liked, "trash," did not help the matter at all.

So the question came up between them of getting something to publish that the people would buy. In this dilemma my friend came to me and asked me if I would write him six songs. I laughed at him a little, but was very happy to do it, my three-years' engagement with Wm. Hall & Son being just out. The songs were finished during vacation, and we tried them over at Willow Farm in manuscript. There were six of us, and I said: "Let us choose from these six songs the one that we think will become most popular. The oldest shall choose first, then the next shall choose from the remainder, then the next, and so on down to the youngest." The youngest was my sister Fanny, then a young girl, and when the choice came to her the only song left unchosen was "Rosalie, the Prairie Flower."

When I took the songs to my friend he said he would prefer to buy them outright. What would I take for the "lot"? There was a bit of sarcasm in the last word. "Well," I replied, "as you propose a wholesale instead of a retail transaction, you shall have the "lot" at wholesale prices, which will be one hundred dollars apiece—six hundred dollars for all." He laughed at the idea. His splendid foreign reprints had cost him nothing. The idea of paying such a sum for these little things could not be thought of. "Very well," I said, "Give me the usual royalty; that will suit me quite as well." This was agreed to, and when he had paid me in royalties nearly three thousand dollars for "Rosalie" alone, he concluded that six hundred for the "lot" would not have been an unreasonable price, especially as all the songs of the set had a fair sale, for which he had to pay in addition. But he learned wisdom by experience as to what people in elementary states must have, and he showed himself an able man and a good musician in the great instruction book that bears his name.

Willow Farm was now headquarters. From there I went to musical conventions in all parts of the country, and there I worked at books and songs. I have said that I never considered that I had a "call" to be a musical composer—that my efforts in that way began by trying to supply my own needs. I can say the same in a still more emphatic way in regard to writing words for music. I presume I should never have attempted to do that if I could always have found some one to do what I wanted. But this I could not do. Sometimes the trouble was with the meter, sometimes with words that followed each other roughly, jolting, like a wagon over a rocky road; sometimes a thin vowel for a high soprano tone, and sometimes wrong emotional expression for the music I had in mind.

My efforts at writing words began in New York, and I well remember how laborious the somewhat mechanical matter of rhyming was at first, and how gradually it grew easier with practice. At North Reading there was no one near to go to for words, but that kind of work was not now so formidable, thanks to the practice I had had, and I enjoyed greatly turning into rhyme for lessons and songs the thoughts that came amid the pleasant scenes that surrounded me there.

The beginning of this kind of work is seen in the "Sabbath Bell," which was the first book to grade carefully lessons and part-songs for singing classes. This was my first venture alone for choirs, singing classes and conventions, and I attribute its success largely to these words, which were written as needed for the grade wanted. The same scenes and surroundings contributed to the singing class department of the "Diapason," which followed. My first sight of the West impressed me strongly, and some songs about the prairies naturally followed. Among the lessons and songs written as above described, some have continued in use to the present time. I mention a few of them here : " By the brooklet clear," "Music everywhere," "High in the summer sky," "O'er prairie, green and fair," "Autumn winds," "O'er the calm lake," "Don't you see me coming?" (song of the bobolink), "Up in the morning so early," "Have you seen my Lillie?" "Ha! ha! ha! Laughing is contagious," "Out on the prairie," "Happy New Year," "Softly she faded," "To the mountain," "On the heather," "Thoughts of childhood" and "Merry May."

While North Reading was headquarters, I was often in New York on my way to or from conventions, and of course in constant communication with my publishers. On one occasion, during the year 1856, Lowell Mason, Jr., the senior partner of the house of Mason Brothers, suggested that I should write a cantata for mixed voices, but on some secular subject. After some consideration haymaking, as it was then carried on, was chosen, and "The Haymakers" decided upon as the title. Mr. Mason (L. M., Jr.) took a great interest in this work, and to a great extent planned it, not only as to characters and action, but as to what, in a general way, each number should be about.

Taking his plan I wrote both words and music—sometimes the words first, sometimes the music first, and sometimes both together. I did most of the work in my new library at Willow Farm, where, by stepping to the door, I could see the very fields in which I had swung the scythe and raked the hay, and in which I had many a time hurried to get the last load into the barn before the thunder-storm should burst upon us. In fact, nearly every scene described in the cantata had its counterpart in my experience on the old farm not many years before, always excepting "Snipkins," the city man who found himself so much out of place in the country and among the haymakers. That was a purely imaginary character. This cantata was published in 1857, and began to be sung immediately. During the following

year I conducted it twenty times in Boston and the neighboring cities.

The second year of the Normal at North Reading had a
still larger attendance. To find boarding-places within a
reasonable distance for all, and to get pianos enough up from
Boston to supply the increasing number who wished to take
private lessons, became a difficult matter, but it was managed,
and the work generally improved with experience. About
this time I tried teaching elementary harmony in classes,
requiring the pupils to know chords through the ear before
writing them. There had been, as I thought, too much *eye*
harmony—deciding that certain harmonies were wrong because they did not look right. Pupils had received the kind
of training that leads to condemning the consecutive fifths
that a skillful composer might use, because, to the eye, they
violated a rule. I had also observed that many harmony
papers that had been given to pupils to fill out with proper
chords were so much Greek to them, so far as hearing in
their minds the chords they were writing; not but that the
teacher might have played the lesson to them as it should
be, but there was no such ear training as made the harmony
a part of the musical life of the pupil.

I found that twenty or thirty could hear and answer as
well as one alone, so I played and they listened until they
could tell promptly and accurately what they heard, beginning, of course, with the simplest combinations. In this training they had nothing to look at, and they wrote only what
had entered their musical minds by the proper avenue, viz.,
the ear. I think the idea of working in this way came to
me from teaching the blind. I found they knew and enjoyed
harmony far more thoroughly than seeing pupils did, and
the result of my experiment was very satisfactory. Instead
of getting tired of harmony and giving it up because they
could not understand it (really because they did not get it),

the class grew more and more interested in their harmony
lessons. I do not remember any approval of Dr. Mason and
Mr. Webb that gave me so much satisfaction and pleasure as
that which came to me on account of this work. Both were
pleased that harmony, which had been a dull and heavy study,
now promised to be a bright and cheery one.

It was interesting to observe the changes that came over
the new pupils during their first three or four weeks in the
Institute. Many of them were great men at home—had been
praised and looked up to until they hardly liked to appear as
if they came as learners. Not infrequently, on being introduced, one would give me a friendly slap on the shoulder
and say : " Well, Root, I thought I would come and see how
you do things here," or, " I should like to show you my way
of teaching," etc. The old hands standing by would look
on mischievously or compassionately, as the case might be,
but generally said nothing to the new-comers about the trials
and tribulations and the " valley of humiliation " which they
would be pretty sure to find before them when they came to
Dr. Mason's searching examination and work, to say nothing
of what would happen to them if their voices or style of
singing were out of true. It was interesting to see how their
self-assertion began to fade out under the criticisms of the
teachers' class, or when they and all in the voice class could
see that the tone they had been producing was wrong.

It was very hard for some of them at first to refrain from
standing on their dignity and arguing the matter, but a few
words from Dr. Mason on the attitude that the true learner
assumes soon opened their eyes. He was very fond of saying : " Except ye become as little children, ye can not enter
into the kingdom of heaven, nor the kingdom of sound, nor
any other kingdom." He used also to say : " Do not waste
time in argument. You are here to get what we have to
give you. Take what you think will be useful ; what you

think will not be, you can reject without saying anything about it." It was very common to see the self-satisfied faces of this kind of new-comers change, first to perplexity, then to anxiety, and finally to discouragement. They were almost certain then to say: " We thought we knew something about music and teaching when we came, but now we see we did not know anything worth speaking of." Then they were told that they had learned the hardest and most important lesson of the session, and from the valley the way would now be pleasant to the sunlight. Dr. Mason often said what he continually exemplified : " Do not be afraid to say ' I do not know.' The teacher who says that to his class will always be believed when he says he does know. Nothing is so dangerous to a teacher's reputation as conceit, and nothing so shuts him out from progress."

All sorts of people came to see us during those summer sessions. Sometimes it was one of Dr. Mason's co-workers in general education, and sometimes musical celebrities, native or foreign. Of the former, Governor Boutwell and Mr. Wm. Russell, the foremost elocutionist of those days, were prominent. These men gave the class many valuable ideas, as well as much enjoyment. A very pleasant gentleman was Mr. Littleton, one of the firm of Novello & Co., of London, who had met Dr. Mason in England, and, being in this country, strayed up to our little town to give him a call.

I took a great deal of interest in those days in the success of my cantatas, which had become so unexpectedly popular. But I remember once thinking that Justice was not the even-handed female she was represented to be, when a gentleman came during one of our sessions to talk with me, as he said, about " The Flower Queen." He was from New England somewhere, but had been teaching in St. Louis, and wound up his year's work by giving that little work. He said : " I have come some miles out of my way to tell you that I have

just cleared a thousand dollars by two performances of your
'Flower Queen' in St. Louis, and the money is here in my
pocket." Then he went on to describe the decorations of
the hall, the enthusiasm of the audience, etc. "How many
singers did you have?" I asked. "Nearly two hundred."
"How many books did you use?" "Oh, they had to com-
mit everything to memory, so I taught the choruses by rote.
I did not need many books—perhaps nine or ten." He
spoke of that as also a matter of credit to himself and of
pleasant interest to me. It evidently did not occur to him
that, while he had made a thousand dollars, the author of
the work had realized the munificent sum of sixty cents, or
thereabout, as his share of the profits. I became used to
that after a while, but this first experience made a strong
impression upon my mind. A law was passed a year or
two later which enabled an author to control the performance of such works, if he chose to take advantage of it. I
tried it awhile with "The Haymakers," but it was more
trouble than it was worth to enforce it, and I soon gave up
the effort.

How true it is that it is only those laws which are upheld
by public opinion that are of real use to us; or, in other
words, it is only those rights that our neighbors say are ours
that we can make available.

The New England boy of fifty years ago remembers that
many of the natural products of the old farm—berries, nuts,
wild fruits, etc.—were practically common property. The
neighbors helped themselves to them as freely as they drank
the water of the springs or breathed the air of the pastures.
Their owners had as undoubted rights to their berries as to
their corn, potatoes or bank notes, and often wished to exercise those rights, but custom and public opinion did not
admit them, and they were helpless—unless, indeed, they
went to law, which the average citizen would rather suffer

than do.   After a while the cranberry began to have a mer-
chantable value, and slowly public opinion changed, until at
last it accorded to owners the same rights to their cranberry
meadows that they had to their corn-fields; but to this day
it is not considered half so bad to gather nuts and huckle-
berries without the owner's knowledge and consent as it is
to take his corn or money.

So it was in early days in regard to music.   We had
each other's compositions for the asking, rather considering
that we were complimenting the author by using them.   We
did not consider that we might be placing an author's works
in injurious competition with himself, and that by advertising
his music in our books we were seizing upon his "good-
will" for our advantage.   It is better now, though the rights
to musical property are not yet as clearly defined as to more
tangible things.

The prominent singers of Boston visited the Normal at
North Reading occasionally, but I do not recall any name
that would be of special interest, unless it would be that of
a large, quiet young man, who was then just beginning his
musical studies, and who, with his teacher, a prominent
choir leader in Boston, passed part of a day with us.   Nobody dreamed that that modest and farmer-like person
would become America's greatest basso, but so it was to be.
I presume I hardly need mention the name of Myron W.
Whitney.

We had many invitations, on one pretext or another, to
go to neighboring towns and sing.   Carriages would be sent
for us, and we should be treated like princes, if we would
consent.   It was pretty hard to resist the pressure from the
inviters on the one side and the invited on the other, for a
majority of the class were always ready for an outing of
that sort.   But we feared the breaking in upon our work
and the distraction that such excursions would cause, and

consented but once. That was at a "commencement" of the Andover Theological Seminary. The professors were great friends of Dr. Mason, and when they urged us to do them this favor we yielded. The procession of all sorts of conveyances that took us the seven miles, up and down half a dozen hills to the mile, our prairie friends will never forget. It is said that the name Andover came from the description people gave of the way there from every point— " over andover andover the hills."

I doubt if such a chorus as we then had is ever heard where people only meet for practice once or twice a week. In the first place, they were practically picked voices. The people who came to us had generally taken to music as a business because they were especially gifted by nature in that way. Then the daily practice of the chorus for so many weeks produced a blending and unanimity that can not be reached in any other way.

The commencement exercises were in the largest church there, and Mr. Webb played the organ. We sang mostly " Messiah " choruses, but a number from the cantata of " Daniel." " How lovely is Zion " came in for a large share of admiration, chiefly, as it seemed to me, because the solo was sung by the best woman that I have ever had the pleasure of being acquainted with. This was the first time that the Normal ever sang away from home, unless upon some of our Saturday excursions to Swan Pond, or some other picnic ground.

CHAPTER XI.

1859–1861, NORTH READING AND CHICAGO—PROMINENT MEM-
BERS OF THE NORMAL INSTITUTE — WRITING AT WILLOW
FARM—OUR SIMPLE MUSIC IN ENGLAND—ROOT AND CADY—
THE CURRENCY — THE GREATER THE REFINEMENT, THE
SMALLER THE COIN—CHICAGO IN 1858—THE "CAMERADE-
RIE" IN A NEW COUNTRY—CONVENTIONS ON THE PRAIRIE—
LAND SHARKS—FIRST ORGAN BOOK—THE FIRST GUN OF THE
WAR.

THE Normal continued its sessions in North Reading
until 1859, and among its members up to this time
were Geo. B. Loomis, for some years superintendent of music in the public schools of Indianapolis, Theodore E. Per-
kins, T. M. Towne, Chester G. Allen, J. M. North, authors
and convention conductors, and Luther W. Mason, for a
long time prominent in the primary department of the
public schools of Boston as musical superintendent and
principal teacher. A few years ago this Mr. Mason went
to Japan, by the invitation of the Japanese government, to
inaugurate there the system of teaching music to children
that had been in use in the Boston schools. He remained
in Tokio about two years, if I remember rightly.

Another member of the North Reading Normal was
Theo. F. Seward, the present energetic leader of the tonic-
sol-fa movement in America. Have you ever received a
letter from Mr. Seward, or read one of his editorials, when
he had his war-paint on for tonic-sol-fa? If so, did not the
handwriting of the one, or the sledge-hammer blows of the
other, give you the idea that he was a giant in size, with the

voice of a stentor? Then have you met him afterward? If so, you found a rather small, delicate-looking man, with a soft voice and a sweet smile, with gentle and refined manners, and one of the kindest hearts in the world—in most respects probably entirely different from your idea. I admire Mr. Seward greatly, but this contrast between his strong, aggressive work and his gentle ways has always to me a humorous side.

Two other members of the Normal Institute in those days, of whom I shall have occasion to speak more at length later, were James R. Murray, the present editor of *The Musical Visitor*, and Chauncey M. Wyman, from Keene, N. H., then just beginning his musical career.

I can not name all the Normals who were successful in their work, for that would include nearly every member from the first session up to the time of which I am writing. They were invariably the strong men and women of their widely varied localities, and their new equipments of methods of teaching and singing gave them great popularity and success.

My time now, from Normal to Normal, was passed in writing at Willow Farm or in conducting musical conventions in various parts of the country. I could easily have occupied every week of the year in the latter work, Mr. Bradbury and I being almost the only prominent people in it for a while. Dr. Mason was occasionally tempted to conduct some of the larger gatherings in New England, but he confined his outside work in those days mostly to the Normal. Mr. Webb was also fully occupied with work in Boston, which he rarely left, but there was now a constant pressure for a book, or a cantata, or songs, so I spent about half the time at my desk. I now began to hear from Mr. Curwen, the elder. He had found my little lessons and part-songs for singing classes helpful in his tonic-sol-fa enterprise in England, and wrote very kind and appreciative letters of acknowledgment for the same. He was accustomed to say, "We have in England plenty of high-class music, and more than enough of the Captain Jinks kind of songs, but there is a wholesome middle-ground in regard to both words and music in which you in America greatly excel," and soon my cantatas and songs were issued there to an extent that I was not fully aware of until a recent visit, when I saw the list of them in the catalogue of the British Museum; but I will speak more fully of that further on. My acquaintance with Mr. Curwen, thus commenced, was kept up by correspondence until his death, and every year revealed to me more and more of his noble and beautiful character.

These were ideal days—writing until noon, and then driving to a neighboring town, or fishing in some of the pretty ponds that were all about us. The favorite fishing ground was a little lake in North Andover, about eight miles away, and many a time have we spent until dark, after our return, distributing to the neighbors the surplus fish of our afternoon's catch.

In 1858 my brother, E. T. Root, and Mr. C. M. Cady started a music business in Chicago—nearly the "far west" in those days—under the firm name of Root & Cady. My convention work brought me occasionally to their neighborhood, and it was an odd and very pleasant sensation to find in this new section a kind of business home. This was not so much on account of the small pecuniary interest I had in the enterprise as the great interest I took in everything my brother did. This brother and myself were nearly of the same age. We had been much together all our lives. He had married the lovely "Lily" of the Rutgers Institute "Flower Queen," and was now preparing for himself a home in the comparatively new city of Chicago. So, whatever applications for conventions I declined, none from the West were refused, and I appeared more and more frequently at the little store.

It was very pleasant to see the new business grow, and it was not long before the partners said: "Come, put in some more capital, and join us; we need the capital, and your name will help us." I was delighted with the idea, not that I thought of giving up my professional work— I did not dream of that, nor of living in Chicago; but to have this connection with my brother, and this business for a kind of recreation, was extremely attractive. So it was soon brought about, and I became a partner in the house of Root & Cady.

Some things that I came in contact with in those days are worth speaking of. One is the currency. Not only you could not use an Illinois bank note in New England, but in going from Boston to New York, or *vice versa*, you had to change your money into that of the state to which you were going. A bank note of either city would be closely scrutinized in the other, and only taken at a discount. As for a western bank note I might almost say it would not be taken in the East at any price. So the returns of my western conventions were always carried home in gold, which it was sometimes hard to get.

To those to whom this seems strange, in the presence of our present national currency, it may be of interest to say that I remember well when there were no such things as dimes and half-dimes, but, instead, the smallest silver coins were in New England "nine-pence" (12½ cents), and "four-pence-half-penny" (6¼ cents). In New York the same coins were called "shilling" and "six-pence." That came from the plan of having a succession of half values from the dollar—50 cts., 25, 12½, and 6¼. Then there were cents and half cents, which were large copper coins.

It is not wonderful that the trouble the fractions caused compelled the present excellent decimal plan. For a year or two perhaps after dimes came in, a difference in value was made between the 10-cent piece and the 12½-cent piece, (and the 5 and 6¼,) but that difference was so troublesome that either by a law or by common consent it was ultimately given up and both were put on a level. Then the old coins, as if mortified and disgusted at being undervalued, retired from public life. For a few years a stray one, looking lonely and antiquated by the side of the bright, new usurper, would occasionally be seen, but they are all gone now, excepting the few, perhaps, that are in the hands of the old coin collectors.

The eagerness with which gold and silver were sought in those times of trouble with bank notes made people anxious and interested in a high degree in regard to the resumption of specie payment, which was suspended during the war and for a time afterward. How good the gold and silver looked in prospect! But when the time for resumption came, everybody waked to the fact that one need of the old times was entirely gone. The new national banking system was in successful operation, and the national bank note of one state was just as good in other states as at home, and at the resumption those who at first loaded themselves with coin soon found that bank notes were far more convenient to carry, and now that they were just as "good as gold," were much to be preferred for the ordinary uses of business. So the millions in coin that were made ready to redeem the national bank notes were practically untouched, and resumption, excepting as it established the value of bank notes, was something of a farce. It was a pretty clear case of the old story of the foreigner and the shaky bank: "If you can pay me, I don't want it; but if you can't pay, I must have it."

It was curious to observe, when specie payment was suspended, how soon all the little coins, as well as the large ones, fled to hiding places.   Then what trouble for change! But that seemed the beginning of success for the horse-car lines, then recently established in Chicago.   People had not become used to them; they had not been well patronized, and were looking rather discouraged—horses, cars and rails. Then the company issued five-cent tickets, which were used for change, not only on the cars but in the stores, and people having a good many of these tickets in their pockets doubled or trebled their car-riding and set the enterprise on its feet.

Then came that most excellent scheme—the government fractional currency—so neat to carry, so very convenient to send by mail; in fact, as much better in every way for ordinary business than the small coin, as bank notes are better than silver dollars. They would have all the advantage now that they had then, and their wearing out and loss by fire, and in other ways, would be a large revenue to the government; but the comparatively few men who sell silver for coinage are powerful enough to deprive us of these advantages, even in the face of the hoarded millions of silver dollars that can not be forced out among the people.

An amusing little incident comes to my mind in connection with this fractional currency.   It was several years that there were practically no coins in Chicago—time enough for a small merchant in newspapers to establish a flourishing business without ever having seen one.   He came into the car to sell his evening papers, and a Californian, sitting next to me, took one and gave him a silver half dime.   The little fellow looked at it, and at the man, and supposing that it was a joke that was being played upon him, thrust the coin back, seized his paper and ran out of the car.   He did not know that the little silver disk was money.   All the five-cent piece he knew was the little paper note for that amount, bearing the government stamp.

Speaking of the five-cent newspaper brings to my mind the fact that for years after I came to Chicago there were no copper coins here. The smallest sum that you could use in paying was five cents. Several efforts to start penny or two-cent papers failed because there were no pennies to pay with, and, of course, no change for a five-cent piece. This fact with regard to new sections of our country is well known, but the deduction from that fact may not be so readily thought of, namely, that where such business conditions exist, society is in a crude and not in a refined state. It is an axiom that the higher the refinement in business transactions the smaller the coin. While in Chicago a half dime was the smallest, in Boston and New York the cent was in common use, in London the half penny, and in Paris the sou, and even the centime. But Chicago has greatly improved. At the present time we are refined enough to have excellent penny and two-cent papers, and no reputable citizen now goes about without copper coins in his pocket.

Looking upon the solid and magnificent streets and drives of Chicago to-day, it is hard to realize their condition in 1858. The first level of the city was but little above the lake, and it was not until some large buildings and blocks of brick and stone had been erected that it was seen that at that level there could be no proper drainage, and that the city—buildings and streets—must be raised several feet. This process was going on when we came. In all the principal thoroughfares some of the buildings were at the new level and some at the old, and progress through them on the side-walk was a constant succession of up and down stairs. Many of the streets were yet unpaved, and although not so bad as a few years before, when in muddy weather the ladies had to be backed up to the stores on carts, the horses or oxen wading knee-deep in mud, still they were sometimes almost impassable. Wood, gravel, stone, and brick all being so far away it was slow and costly work to make the improvements required by the peculiar location of this extraordinary city. After the fire, the opportunity was taken to raise the grade still higher in rebuilding, so that now it is entirely satisfactory in that respect.

The *camaraderie*, or "hail fellow well met" feeling in a new country is one of its most striking features. People from different social grades in the older settled places of the East meet here on a level. Social distinctions are in nobody's way, for there are none, and the best man wins. One of my early conventions in the West was in such a community. On one of Illinois' great prairies, where eighteen months before there was but a railroad shanty, there were now fifteen hundred people.

They were all young and energetic—just the kind to leave the quieter East and enjoy the excitement of starting a new town. An unusual proportion were from cities where they had been members of choirs and musical societies, and they thought a musical convention in the midst of their bustle and building would be a pleasant novelty. We held our sessions in a hall over a large store, and our final concert in an unfinished church edifice, seats being improvised of the building material for the occasion. A few "prairie schooners" (as certain long wagons were called) brought singers from distant prairie homes, and a few came on the railroad from places still farther away, but from the town itself was a larger proportion of cultivated and refined singers than I ever found in a country convention at the East. L. W. Wheeler, who has been for some years one of Boston's most popular voice teachers, was one of the tenors of that convention, and, although just beginning then, gave unmistakable signs of the voice and talent which have since made him so successful.

This town was Kewanee, now one of our finest inland places. I was laughing at one of the men of that convention about the way they were hurrying up their houses, when he said: "Oh, that's nothing to the way they did at first in Chicago. There a man would say to the only carpenter they had, 'I believe I'll settle here; when can you build me a house?' and the answer would be, 'Well, there's Smith, Monday; Jones, Tuesday; Brown, Wednesday; Johnson, Thursday; I'll put yours up Friday.'" Of course this was all burlesque, but it does not give a bad idea of the way things are done while people are roughing it in a new country.

I have often thought that a romance might be written, embodying some of the early real estate transactions of Chicago that would be of intense interest. The only trouble would be that some of the events would be considered too extravagant even for fiction. One story is told of an emigrant—a Hollander, who, with his family, landed in Chicago from a sailing craft before the first railroad had reached so far, and was immediately set upon by "land sharks," as some of the early real estate dealers were called, and finally persuaded to give six hundred dollars for some low land by the river that would then have been considered dear at one-fifth the price. Some of the less hardened of the real estate brotherhood were disposed to protest against the outrageous swindle, but the old fellow seemed satisfied. He took some gold and silver from his pouch and leather belt, and his wife and children cut out coins that had been sewed up in their clothing, and he paid the money. He put up a shanty at once, and then commenced preparing his land for vegetables by processes that he had been familiar with at home. His wife and children helped. He sold his produce readily, and had no difficulty in getting a living after his fashion. Pretty soon people began to build around him, and he was occasionally asked if he did not want to sell his place. No; what should he want to sell for?—he would only have to go and get another place for a vegetable garden, and that was too much trouble. By and by the pressure grew stronger, and the offers got up into the thousands. No; he had built a frame house now, and wasn't going to move. Then the increased taxes, and some assessments for town improvements were too much for his little savings, and he sold a small end of his domain. But this brought him so much money that the surplus made him feel that he should never need any more, so he resisted all offers and importunities, and kept on with his vegetable garden as long as he lived. Then his heirs sold the place for nearly a million dollars.

This playing at business (for I did nothing of the buying or selling), and the new and adventurous life of Chicago were so attractive to me that early in 1859 I took a room in the building in which the store was, and occupied it as a library and working-room between convention engagements. Not long before, Mr. Henry Mason, the youngest brother of my publishers, had formed a copartnership with Mr. Hamlin, under the firm name of Mason & Hamlin, for the manufacture of melodeons. They prospered, and soon called their larger instruments harmoniums, and not long after, cabinet organs. Some time in 1862 the Masons asked me if I thought I could make an instruction book for these instruments. I said I would try, and the result was "The School for the Harmonium and Cabinet Organ." This was my first work of importance in my new quarters. It was published by Mason Brothers, and had a large sale. It inaugurated a much better graded method than any previous book had contained, and I have sometimes thought that the copyright laws would be more just if they included the plan as well as

the contents of a book of that kind. But there being no
such protection, my plan has been generally adopted by
reed organ instructors ever since.

In 1860 the Normal was held in Chicago, Dr. Mason, Mr.
Bradbury, and myself principal teachers. By this time other
Normals were started by those who had been with us, and
we no longer occupied the entire field. Still, the interest in
that kind of school having increased, our attendance continued to be large. I have no list of that class, but I recall
that among its successful members was N. Coe Stewart, the
present superintendent of music in the public schools of
Cleveland, Ohio.

My family was still at Willow Farm, excepting F. W.,
who was now old enough to be away at boarding school, and
I had no thought, yet, of another home. However, the little
business was improving and I enjoyed more and more being
in the neighborhood of its small whirl. I might, perhaps,
have foreseen that if it continued to increase, the whirl might
eventually grow large enough to include me in its round of
hard and confining work, but I did not. I went and came
—was free to work in my pleasant room or to be off at conventions, now in New England, now in New York or Pennsylvania, or the West—not a moment hung heavily on my
hands. Then we began to publish a little. First a song or
two, and some instrumental pieces in sheet form. After a
while we decided to venture on a book, and put in hand one
that I was then working on for day-schools; but now the
WAR burst upon us!

What a change came over the whole country when that
momentous event was announced! How the bustling, cheery
life of Chicago became suddenly grave and serious. With
what different eyes we saw everything about us. It was not
the same sunshine that made the city so bright yesterday,
and these were not the same faces of neighbors that then

nodded so light-heartedly as they passed. The old flag had been fired upon, and that act had waked into stern determination the patriotism of every loyal heart.

CHAPTER XII.

1861–1870, CHICAGO—WRITING THE WAR SONGS—SOME INCI-
DENTS CONCERNING THEM—HENRY C. WORK—P. P. BLISS—
"THE SONG MESSENGER OF THE NORTH-WEST"—THE ORI-
GIN OF "TRAMP"—GROWTH OF BUSINESS—JAMES R. MUR-
RAY AND "DAISY DEANE"—B. R. HANBY—CARYL FLORIO—
DR. MASON'S LAST NORMAL—THE NORMAL AT SOUTH BEND,
IND.—THE ORIGIN OF "NATIONAL NORMAL"—CARLO BAS-
SINI.

IN common with my neighbors I felt strongly the gravity
of the situation, and while waiting to see what would be
done, wrote the first song of the war. It was entitled "The
first gun is fired, may God protect the right." Then at every
event, and in all the circumstances that followed, where I
thought a song would be welcome, I wrote one. And here
I found my fourteen years of extemporizing melodies on the
blackboard, before classes that could be kept in order only by
prompt and rapid movements, a great advantage. Such work
as I could do at all I could do quickly. There was no waiting for a melody. Such as it was it came at once, as when
I stood before the blackboard in the old school days.

I heard of President Lincoln's second call for troops one
afternoon while reclining on a lounge in my brother's house.
Immediately a song started in my mind, words and music
together:

> "Yes, we'll rally round the flag, boys, we'll rally once again,
>   Shouting the battle-cry of freedom!"

I thought it out that afternoon, and wrote it the next morning at the store. The ink was hardly dry when the Lum-

bard brothers—the great singers of the war—came in for something to sing at a war meeting that was to be holden immediately in the court-house square just opposite. They went through the new song once, and then hastened to the steps of the court-house, followed by a crowd that had gathered while the practice was going on. Then Jule's magnificent voice gave out the song, and Frank's trumpet tones led the refrain—

" The Union forever, hurrah, boys, hurrah! "

and at the fourth verse a thousand voices were joining in the chorus. From there the song went into the army, and the testimony in regard to its use in the camp and on the march, and even on the field of battle, from soldiers and officers, up to generals, and even to the good President himself, made me thankful that if I could not shoulder a musket in defense of my country I could serve her in this way.

Many interesting war incidents were connected with these songs. The one that moved me most was told by an officer who was in one of the battles during the siege of Vicksburg. He said an Iowa regiment went into the fight eight hundred strong, and came out with a terrible loss of more than half their number; but the brave fellows who remained were waving their torn and powder-stained banner, and singing

"Yes, we'll rally round the flag, boys."

Some years after, at the closing concert of a musical convention in Anamosa, Iowa, I received a note, saying, " If the author of ' The Battle-cry of Freedom ' would sing that song it would gratify several soldiers in the audience who used to sing it in the army." I read the request to the audience, and said I would willingly comply with it, but first would like to relate an incident concerning one of their Iowa regiments. Then I told the above about the battle near Vicks-

burg. When I finished I noticed a movement at the end of
the hall, and an excited voice cried out, " Here is a soldier
who lost his arm in that battle." I said, " Will he come forward and stand by me while I sing the song?" A tall, fine-
looking man, with one empty sleeve, came immediately to
my side, and I went through it, he joining in the chorus.
But it was hard work. I had to choke a good deal, and
there was hardly a dry eye in the house. He was teaching
school a few miles from there, and was quite musical. I
sent him some music after I returned to Chicago, and kept
up the acquaintance by correspondence for some time.

The following from *The Century*, published a year or two
ago, will be of interest in this connection:

UNION WAR SONGS AND CONFEDERATE OFFICERS.

The reading of Mr. Brander Matthews' " Songs of the War," in
the August number of *The Century*, vividly recalls to mind an incident of my own experience, which seems to me so apt an illustration
of the effect of army songs upon men that I venture to send it to you,
as I remember it, after twenty-five years.

A day or two after Lee's surrender in April, 1865, I left our ship
at Dutch Gap, in the James river, for a run up to Richmond, where I
was joined by the ship's surgeon, the paymaster and one of the junior
officers. After " doing " Richmond pretty thoroughly we went in the
evening to my rooms for dinner. Dinner being over, and the events
of the day recounted, the doctor, who was a fine player, opened the
piano, saying: " Boys, we've got our old quartet here; let's have a
sing." As the house opposite was occupied by paroled Confederate
officers no patriotic songs were sung. Soon the lady of the house
handed me this note:

" Compliments of General —— and staff. Will the gentlemen
kindly allow us to come over and hear them sing?"

Of course we consented, and they came. As the General entered
the room, I recognized instantly the face and figure of one who stood
second only to Lee or Jackson in the whole Confederacy. After in-
troductions and the usual interchange of civilities we sang for them
glee and college songs, until at last the General said:

" Excuse me, gentlemen; you sing delightfully; but what we

want to hear is your army songs." Then we gave them the army songs with unction—the "Battle Hymn of the Republic," "John Brown's Body," "We're Coming, Father Abraham," "Tramp, Tramp, Tramp, the Boys are Marching," through the whole catalogue to the "Star-Spangled Banner"—to which many a foot beat time as if it had never stepped to any but the "music of the Union"—and closed our concert with "Rally Round the Flag, Boys."

When the applause had subsided, a tall, fine-looking fellow, in a major's uniform, exclaimed: "Gentlemen, if we'd had your songs we'd have whipped you out of your boots! Who couldn't have marched or fought with such songs? We had nothing, absolutely nothing, except a bastard 'Marseillaise,' the 'Bonny Blue Flag' and 'Dixie,' which were nothing but jigs. 'Maryland, My Maryland' was a splendid song, but the old 'Lauriger Horatius' was about as inspiring as the 'Dead March in Saul,' while every one of the Yankee songs is full of marching and fighting spirit." Then turning to the General, he said: "I shall never forget the first time I heard 'Rally Round the Flag.' 'Twas a nasty night during the 'Seven Days' Fight,' and if I remember rightly it was raining. I was on picket, when, just before 'taps,' some fellow on the other side struck up that song and others joined in the chorus until it seemed to me the whole Yankee army was singing. Tom B——, who was with me, sung out, 'Good heavens, Cap, what are those fellows made of, anyway? Here we've licked 'em six days running, and now on the eve of the seventh they're singing, 'Rally Round the Flag.' I am not naturally superstitious, but I tell you that song sounded to me like the 'knell of doom,' and my heart went down into my boots; and though I've tried to do my duty, it has been an uphill fight with me ever since that night."

The little company of Union singers and Confederate auditors, after a pleasant and interesting interchange of stories of army experiences, then separated, and as the General shook hands at parting, he said to me: "Well, the time *may* come when we can *all* sing the 'Star-Spangled Banner' again." I have not seen him since.

The following extract from a letter recently received also belongs here:

I was lately much interested in an incident, as given in "Bright Skies and Dark Shadows," Dr. Henry M. Field's last book, just published. This incident took place on the day of the great battle of Franklin, near Nashville, Tenn., and was told Mr. Field on the battle-field by a Mr. McEwen, an old resident of Nashville, at whose house General Kimball made his headquarters, and from whose front door Mr. McEwen witnessed the whole battle, which was fought during the latter part of the day.

"About four o'clock, after the General had left for the field, there lingered a Colonel, from Indianapolis, in my parlor, who asked my daughters to sing and play a piece of music. My daughters asked what they should play. He replied that he did not know one piece of music from another, except field music. I spoke and asked the young ladies to sing and play a piece which had recently come out, 'Just before the battle, mother.' At my request they sat down and sang, and when about half through, as I stepped to the door, a shell exploded within fifty yards. I immediately returned and said, 'Colonel, if I am any judge, it is just about that time now!' He immediately sprang to his feet and ran in the direction of his regiment, but before he reached it, or about that time, he was shot, the bullet passing quite through him. He was taken to Nashville, and eighteen days after, I received a message from him through an officer, stating the fact of his being shot, and that the piece of music the young ladies were executing was still ringing in his ears, and had been ever since he left my parlor the evening of the battle. In April, four months later, after the war was over, he had sufficiently recovered to travel, when he came to Franklin, as he stated, expressly to get the young ladies to finish the song, and relieve his ears. His wife and more than a dozen officers accompanied him. He found the ladies, and they sang and played the piece through for him in the presence of all the officers, and they wept like children."

If you have made any music that will ring for four months in the ears of a person that doesn't know one tune from another, I thought you ought to know it.

As I have said, when anything happened that could be voiced in a song, or when the heart of the Nation was moved by particular circumstances or conditions caused by the war, I wrote what I thought would then express the emotions of the soldiers or the people. Picturing the condition and thoughts of the soldier on the eve of an engagement, I wrote "Just before the battle, mother" and "Within the sound of the enemy's guns." When our brave Colonel Mulligan fell, his last words were "Lay me down and save the flag." The day after the news of that event reached us, the song bearing that title was issued. It was much sung at the time in remembrance of that distinguished and lamented officer. I tried to help the enlistments by "Come, brothers, all, 'tis Columbia's call," and to hit the copperhead element of the North by "Stand up for Uncle Sam, boys." I voiced the feeling of the people in regard to the treatment of prisoners by "Starved in prison," and gave a more hopeful view in "Tramp, tramp, tramp, the boys are marching." "O, come you from the battle-field?" and "Brother, tell me of the battle" represented the anxiety of those who had fathers or sons or brothers in the army, and "The Vacant Chair" the mourning for the lost one. One of the thrilling scenes of the war is described in "Who'll Save the Left?" and the grief of the Nation at the death of President Lincoln by "Farewell, father, friend and guardian." This is a partial list of the songs that I wrote during the war. Only a few had an extended use and popularity, but none was entirely useless.

One day early in the war a quiet and rather solemn-looking young man, poorly clad, was sent up to my room from the store with a song for me to examine. I looked at it and then at him in astonishment. It was "Kingdom Coming," —elegant in manuscript, full of bright, good sense and comical situations in its "darkey" dialect—the words fitting the melody almost as aptly and neatly as Gilbert fits Sullivan— the melody decidedly good and taking, and the whole exactly suited to the times. "Did you write this—words and music?" I asked. A gentle "Yes" was the answer. "What is your business, if I may inquire?" "I am a printer." "Would you rather write music than set type?" "Yes." "Well, if this is a specimen of what you can do, I think you may give up the printing business." He liked that idea very much, and an arrangement with us was soon made. He needed some musical help that I could give him, and we needed just such songs as he could write. The connection, which continued some years, proved very profitable both to him and to us. This was Henry C. Work, whose principal songs while he was with us were "Kingdom Coming," "Babylon is Fallen," "Wake, Nicodemus," "Ring the Bell, Watchman," "Song of a Thousand Years," "Marching Thro' Georgia" and "Come Home, Father."

Mr. Work was a slow, pains-taking writer, being from one to three weeks upon a song; but when the work was done it was like a piece of fine mosaic, especially in the fitting of words to music. His "Marching Thro' Georgia" is more played and sung at the present time than any other song of the war. This is not only on account of the intrinsic merit of its words and music, but because it is *retrospective*. Other war songs, "The Battle-cry of Freedom" for example, were for exciting the patriotic feeling on *going in* to the war or the battle; "Marching Thro' Georgia" is a glorious remembrance on coming triumphantly out, and so has been more appropriate to soldiers' and other gatherings ever since.

It must have been some time in 1863 that I received a letter from somewhere in Pennsylvania that interested us all very much. It accompanied the manuscript of a song. Would we give the writer a flute for it, was the substance of the letter, expressed in a quaint and original way, and in beautiful handwriting. We were on the lookout for bright men, and we felt sure that here was one. The song needed some revising, but we took it and sent him the flute. After a while he wrote again, saying he would like to come out to Chicago if he could find anything to do. He gave an account of his accomplishments in his droll way, and we all became much interested in having him come. I think it was he who

finally made the plan that was agreed upon, namely: He
would go as our representative to the towns that would
naturally be tributary to Chicago, and hold conventions, or
give concerts, or do something musical, whenever he could
get the opportunity, (his wife being his accompanist,) and so
turn people's attention to us for whatever they might want
in the way of music.   For this service we guaranteed him a
certain annual sum.   If the proceeds of his concerts and
conventions did not reach that amount we were to make it
up.   While engaged in this work he was constantly sending
in words and music of various kinds for revision and correction.   It was not long before I saw that here was a man who
had a "call" especially as a poet.   His musical training and
experiences were too limited to permit safe flights on his part
beyond simple harmonies, although it was easily seen that
he had a natural vein of true melody.   What a wonderful use
his songs have performed now for more than a score of years.
I presume it is seen that I am writing of the beloved and
lamented P. P. Bliss.

When Mr. Moody, from being a simple, hard working
but devoted city missionary in Chicago, began to come to
the front as an evangelist, Mr. Bliss's songs, and some that I
wrote, were of much use to him.   He used to say of my first
gospel song, "Come to the Savior," that it was the "Rally
Round the Flag" of the gospel work.   It was indeed stirring
when Mr. Bliss's magnificent voice gave it forth, for it then
came from a heart and soul in deepest sympathy with the
work to which he ultimately devoted himself—the writing
and singing of gospel songs.   He remained with us until the
breaking up caused by the great fire, and we published all
the songs and other music that he wrote up to that time.

The growth of our business after the war commenced
was something remarkable.   The name of Root & Cady
went all over the land on our war songs, and on our little

musical monthly, *The Song Messenger of the Northwest.*
Those among the people and in the army who liked our
publications seemed to turn to us for everything they wanted
in our line when it was possible. We kept everything in
the way of musical merchandise from pianos and organs to
jewsharps, and all the music of the day in book or sheet
form. My brother attended to the business detail in all the
departments, Mr. Cady to the finances and general management, and I to the publications. My brother William was
also with us in the office.

Speaking of *The Song Messenger* reminds me of an incident that may be worth mentioning. We published a New
Year's extra in those days which we sent broadcast from
Maine to—I was going to say Georgia, but that section was
barred out then. We sent from the North and West as far
South as we could. I think we were the first to send " To
the principal singer," etc., and the plan being new the little
missives were not thrown into the waste basket to any extent, either by postmasters or recipients, but produced great
results. I used to write a song for this extra. The year
previous to the time of which I am speaking, " Just before
the battle, mother," was the song. December was now approaching, and I was very much interested in something I
was working at—" The Curriculum," I think it was—and had
put off the song for the coming extra. One day my brother
said, " We must have that song or we can not get the paper
into the hands of the people by New Year's Day ; go write
it now while it is on your mind." In two hours I brought
him the song. We tried it over and he said, " I must con-
fess I don't think much of it, but it may do." I was inclined
to agree with him about the music, but after all was a little
disappointed, because I had grown quite warm and interested
in writing the words. They were on a subject that was then
very near the hearts of the loyal people of the North. The

song was "Tramp, tramp, tramp, the boys are marching," and was not only an illustration of the advantage of my blackboard training, but was a further confirmation of what I have said before, that in my case successes were usually surprises.

In 1863, having outgrown our quarters on Clark street, we moved into the Crosby Opera-house building, then just erected on Washington street, near State. This store and basement were one hundred and eighty feet long by thirty in width, to which was eventually added a building just across the alley in the rear, which aggregated a still larger floor area. The basement in this rear building was occupied by our printing-office and steam presses, and the main floor by pianos and organs. The second story had rooms for band and orchestra instruments and "small goods," and one fitted up for my use. Here I made my books and songs, and looked after the publishing interests of the house. This large amount of room was necessitated by the buying out of various small musical establishments, culminating in the purchase of the extensive catalogue, with all its music plates, of the entire stock of Henry Tolman & Co., of Boston— two or three car loads. This catalogue included that of Nathan Richardson, afterwards Russell & Richardson, and afterwards Russell & Tolman. So the songs of mine that they had published came back to me, and I was now their publisher as well as author.

When "The Battle-cry of Freedom" came out I sent, as usual, the first copy to my wife, who was still at North Reading. Soon after she received it she learned that James R. Murray, one of our Normal boys, to whom we were much attached, had volunteered, and was then in camp at Lynn-field, the next town east, so she and my father determined to go and give him a "God speed" before he went to the front. They did so, and gave him the new song, which he introduced into that section of the army. While in Virginia, in his second year of service, Mr. Murray wrote and sent us " Daisy Deane," a beautiful song, which, doubtless, some of my readers will remember. It was one of the marked successes of the day. We kept up a constant correspondence, and I saw not only his musical abilities, but unmistakable signs of his editorial capabilities. So when he left the army he came to us as editor of *The Song Messenger*, and assistant in the writing and publishing department of our business.

There came to us in those days a very interesting and talented man by the name of Hanby. He was educated for the ministry, but was so strongly inclined to music that he decided to try to make that his life's work. He had already written " Darling Nelly Gray," which was published by O. Ditson & Co., and which had a large sale. He was also the author of " Ole Shady," which is famous still. He wrote while with us some beautiful Sunday-school songs, some of which are in use yet. But he died almost at the commencement of his career.

I must not omit to speak in this connection of Chauncey M. Wyman, whom I have mentioned as one of the North Reading normals, and who cast in his lot with us in those days. He had used my books in his convention work in the East, and had attended some conventions that I conducted in Vermont and New Hampshire. In one he was assistant conductor, and I saw that he was one of the coming men. So when he decided that he would have a book of his own I asked him to come out to Chicago and make it, and we would publish it. This he did, and " The Palm " was the result. What he would have done as a composer can hardly be told by this one effort, but as a conductor I have no hesitation in saying that he would have stood in the highest rank had he lived. His magnetism was wonderful, and his control of a chorus absolute. What he wished to accomplish he did, if the capacities of the singers were equal to his conceptions. I have a very tender feeling when I think of the great Normal (of which I will speak later), where he was our oratorio conductor, and from which he went to his New England home never to leave it alive. His calm exterior gave no hint of the intense strain he was under on that memorable occasion in the introduction and use of his first book and the conducting of our great chorus. We also published the early, if not the first works of H. R. Palmer—"The Song Queen," "The Song King," "The Normal Collection," and "Palmer's Concert Choruses."

Among the incidents in regard to people who became connected with us in those days I must not omit this: One day a delicate and refined looking, but poorly clad young man came to the office, which was in the center of the store and where I happened to be, and said: "I am a musician, and wish employment. I have been in a theatrical company which has disbanded in Indiana, and my trunk is detained there. I am entirely without means, but I can play, I can read well at sight, and I can compose, as I will show you." All this was said with the utmost fluency, after which he stepped lightly to a piano and played an Etude elegantly. He then asked for pen and music paper, and wrote without the slightest hesitation or delay a song, words and music. I do not know why I did not think that last performance a pretense, for the work was as elegant as his playing, but I did not. There was something about him that made us all feel that under that airy manner there was solid musical attainment, and that he was all he pretended to be. That proved true, and he was with us a year or two. He was then W. J. Robjohn, but is at present known as Caryl Florio, one of New York's most accomplished musicians.

When our business began to assume the large proportions that it afterward reached, I saw that it could no longer be regarded as a secondary matter or a recreation. It was clear that I was to be absorbed in its whirl as my hard-working brother had been from the beginning. My department now demanded nearly all the time I could spare from writing, and to attend to that properly I must give up conventions, and, consequently, Willow Farm as home. So in 1863 I moved my family to Chicago. It consisted then of wife, two sons, and three daughters. F. W., the oldest, had taken lessons upon the piano from Mr. B. C. Blodgett, now one of the most prosperous musical men of Massachusetts, and then he had studied for a while with Mr. William Mason in New York. He took an organist's situation as soon as he arrived in Chicago, and divided his time between the store and practice. When my second son finished his school studies in Chicago both boys went to Europe, and studied music and languages in Germany and Italy for a year or more. On their return, F. W. decided to make music his profession, and Charles went into the store.

Early in the war, probably in 1862, the last Normal in which Dr. Mason taught was held in Wooster, Ohio. Dr. Mason, myself, and Geo. B. Loomis were the principal teachers, and the work continued six weeks. There was a good attendance, but the recruiting officers around us, and an occasional war meeting kept up an excitement that worked against us, not only in other people's minds but in our own. We were deeply interested in the struggle, and always ready to help at the war meetings. The new war-songs contributed not a little to rouse the enthusiasm of the people and help the recruiting, sung as they were by our fine chorus. Phillip Phillips, I remember, was one of the normals of that session.

When the war began no one thought it would last long —a year was the outside limit in most minds, but in the second year the magnitude of the undertaking began to appear. So many young men of the North were in the army that I made no more attempts to hold the Normal until the war was over. Then I think the first one was in Winona, Minnesota. I was the principal, but the younger men were now coming to the front, and I had excellent assistants in Bliss, Towne, F. W. (before he went abroad), and O. D. Adams. J. R. Murray was left in charge of my department of the business in Chicago. At the next Normal H. R. Palmer and I joined forces. It was held in Janesville, Wis., and was a large and interesting gathering.

But the most memorable Normal session of those days was held in South Bend, Indiana, in 1870. Dr. Mason and Mr. Webb had left the work to younger hands. Mr. Bradbury had passed away, and I was alone of the original four. I secured the services of Carlo Bassini, then well known and extremely popular throughout the United States, as the voice teacher, and William Mason, the distinguished pianist, not only to give lessons to advanced pupils, but to give recitals and lectures twice a week to the entire Institute. These recitals inaugurated a new department in Normal work, which has been kept up ever since. Chauncey M. Wyman, of whom I have spoken, was our chorus and oratorio conductor, and Bliss, Towne, and F. W. Root (just returned from Europe) assisted in various departments. W. S. B. Mathews, of Chicago, was Mr. Mason's assistant in piano teaching. I think it was here that C. C. Case and James McGranahan made their first appearance as Normal pupils. S. W. Straub was also a member this year.

Schuyler Colfax, then Vice-President of the United States, lived in South Bend, and was very fond of looking in upon us, and on one occasion I asked him to say something to the class. He first wanted to know how many were in attendance. I told him about two hundred from abroad. (I believe there were one hundred and eighty actual teachers and those intending to teach.) He then wanted to know how many States were represented, and asked the members from the different States to raise their hands as he named their State. This was done, and it was found that *seventeen* States and Canada were represented in the membership of the Institute. Then Mr. Colfax commenced his speech by saying: "This should be called 'The National Musical Institute,' since the nation is so largely represented in it," and I was glad to adopt that designation, as "Normals" had now sprung up all over the land.

The evening chorus was a noble one, numbering nearly three hundred singers. The oratorio was the "Creation," and at the first rehearsal Mr. Wyman tried several of the choruses, among them "The Heavens are Telling," to ascertain the reading ability of his class. The choruses were not well sung, but there was no breakdown. They were read straight through. Mr. Bassini, who was present, expressed some surprise that people from such widely varied localities should have all sung the "Creation." I told him they had probably never seen it before. This he could not believe. I then asked all who had sung "The Heavens are Telling" before to rise, and four persons stood up. "Ah," said Mr. Bassini, in his demonstrative way, "I was for many years chorus master for the Italian opera in different countries of Europe and in South America, and I never found people who could read like that." "How did you teach them?" I asked. "Oh, I played the part they were to sing over and over on my violin until they learned it. It was great drudgery." Recalling that incident reminds me that Mr. Bassini came to this country as a solo violinist. I heard him in that capacity in New York in '46 or '47. He did not succeed in that line, although he played finely, and for a time he went out of sight. Then he began to be known as a teacher of singing, and from that time no one ever heard of him as a violinist. He knew well the value of having but one specialty. In this he became famous, and made a great deal of money. He cleared over a thousand dollars in his six weeks with us at South Bend. But he was a delicate man. It was only his indomitable will that kept his frail body up to the work he did. He went to Chicago from South Bend to teach in a short Normal that Mr. Palmer was holding, and was there my guest. But he could not stay through. He left the second week, and went home to die. He was a most lovable man, and is remembered with warm affection by us all.

CHAPTER XIII.

1871–1873, CHICAGO—THE HEALTH LIFT AND THE ASTONISHED
PIANO MOVERS—THE GIGANTIC LOTTERY SCHEME—OUR
SUCCESSFUL PUBLICATIONS, INCLUDING DR. PALMER'S AND
MR. BLISS'S EARLY WORKS—HEAVY STOCK—THE GREAT
FIRE—MY GREEN BOX—MR. CURWEN'S GIFT—NEW BUSI-
NESS ARRANGEMENTS—THE NORMAL OF '72—THE SAD
TELEGRAM.

WHEN my convention work was at its height, and I
about thirty-eight years of age, I used to have occasionally a nervous re-action at the close of my four days'
work that affected my head unpleasantly. When our increasing business confined me more, and some large obligations that were upon us made me anxious, the trouble came
oftener and each time remained longer. Finally it came to
stay. The doctors said it was a trouble of the brain, and I
must quit business—had better go to Europe, or somewhere
away. About that time Mr. Curwen (the elder), hearing that
I was out of health, invited me to make him a visit. He
wrote that if I would come they would welcome me to London with a chorus of five thousand voices singing my music.
But I had not the courage to face the sea voyage and declined.

Being near Boston not long after, a medical friend said:
"Try Butler; they say he has done wonders for such cases
as yours." "Who is Butler?" "Oh, he is a man who has
an apparatus for lifting—says he can make people so strong
that they can lift away all troubles that flesh is heir to." I
could see that my friend had not unqualified confidence in

the scheme, or, rather, that he had the usual professional distrust of anything out of the regular line; but drowning men catch at straws, so I tried it. I booked myself for three months of lifting iron weights. I went once a day, occupying about half an hour each time in making four lifts. Nothing could be more simple—standing erect upon a table, bending the knees, grasping a handle which was attached to a bar, upon which weights were hung under the table, and then straightening up. The act was a matter of a few seconds, but it sent the blood to every capillary of the body. As the strength increased the weights were increased. The third week I was inclined to be discouraged, for I did not feel any better. If anything, my troubles were sharper and more pronounced; but Mr. Butler smiled his imperturbable smile, and said: "Can you lift more than you could last week?" "Yes." "Are you absolutely sure of that?" "Yes; there can be no doubt about that; there are the iron weights to prove it." "Then, no matter how you feel, you are better." This bolstered me up and I went on. I required this kind of help several times before the three months were out. My troubles had been years in coming on, and were not to be driven away in a few weeks. But before the three months were out I saw that I was on the right track, so I purchased a set of the apparatus and had it sent to my house in Chicago. There I continued its use, and in six months I began to work a little.

After a while it got noised about that I was lifting heavy weights. Our piano movers were specially interested in what was said. I was still rather pale, and certainly did not look like a person who could lift such weights as they prided themselves upon lifting, so they were entirely skeptical on the subject. They said nothing to me, but were disposed to be facetious about the matter among themselves, as I was told. One day they had occasion to move a piano to my

house, and I said, " Boys, would you like to try the lift?"
They assented eagerly, and followed me up into the attic,
where I had a room arranged for the apparatus.   I showed
them what to do, and put on a moderate weight which they
all lifted in turn.   There were three of them.   Then I added
more, and continued until they began to give out.   The
youngest, who was a very strong lad of twenty, just strug-
gled up with six hundred.   Then I added another hundred
and lifted it without difficulty.   Their astonishment and con-
sternation were amusing.   There must be some trick about
it.   But no ; there were the iron disks, weighing fifty pounds
each, which they could take into their hands, and fourteen
of them were on the bar.   I did not explain to them that I
probably could not have lifted in a stooping position what
they did, nor that while certain of their muscles used in that
position were very strong, certain others, when they stood
straight, were not up to the mark, and when the strain came
equally on all, the weak ones gave way, just as a chain in
use would only be as strong as its weakest link.   They never
could understand it, and looked at me with awe and wonder
after that, whenever I passed them in the store or on the
street.

In a year and a half I could lift more than a thousand
pounds, and my troubles were gone.   Meanwhile my partners
and others tried it and were benefited, and we furnished the
capital to start a room where the system could be adminis-
tered to the public, and Dr. Frank W. Reilly was placed in
charge.   He called the establishment the " Health Lift," and
made some important improvements in the apparatus, and
gave a clear and rational statement of the reasons for its
success.   This was among the prosperous enterprises swept
away by the great fire.

A curious episode in our opera-house life is worth relating.   Somewhere about '69 Mr. Crosby, under some financial

pressure, put up his magnificent building as the prize in a gigantic lottery scheme. One hundred thousand tickets at five dollars apiece were to be sold, and the holder of the successful one was to own the opera-house—one chance in one hundred thousand. Tickets were sold all over the United States, and it was almost a national affair when the time for drawing came. At all events the excitement in and about the building was intense. I was not present when the drawing took place, but I think it was done by a child blindfolded, the tickets having been thoroughly stirred up in a revolving cylinder. The winner was a miller in southern Illinois, but he was immediately induced, under the fear that the whole proceeding might be found to be illegal, to take a much less sum than five hundred thousand dollars for his prize. But what he did receive made him a rich man. He came into the store after the matter was all settled, and, looking about, remarked, " I owned all this for half an hour." In the course of the conversation he said, " I knew I should win ; I always do." Then he gave some account of his successes at fairs and raffles in St. Louis, near which city he lived, which, if true, were certainly very remarkable. I think the building went back into Mr. Crosby's hands.

Up to 1871 we had published of my composition the war songs before mentioned, and a good many others on various subjects, and of books " The Silver Lute," " The Bugle Call," " Chapel Gems," " The Musical Fountain," " The Forest Choir," " The Prize," " The Coronet," " The Triumph," and " The Musical Curriculum." On my works we had both author's and publisher's profit. On those of other authors, for whom we published, we had only the publisher's profit, as on them we paid royalties.

When the war closed the war songs stopped as if they had been shot. Everybody had had enough of war. " Tramp " was the last successful one, and had but a short life—less than a year, but in that time our profit on it was ten thousand dollars. All the songs by Mr. Work and myself, that have been mentioned, had large sales, the above giving some general idea of the profit of each to author and publisher. Of " The Silver Lute " (for day schools) were sold more than a hundred thousand copies. "The Prize," for Sunday schools, was still more successful. " The Triumph," which was the last successful large-sized book for choirs and conventions ($13.50 a dozen), sold ninety thousand copies the first year, at a profit to us of thirty thousand dollars. H. R. Palmer made the first successful smaller-sized books for singing classes and conventions—the " Song Queen " and the " Song King," both of which had very large sales, and contributed proportionately to our profits. All the other books by Mr. Palmer and myself, as well as those by Mr. Bliss, that we published, were fairly successful. My largest work, "The Musical Curriculum," had been but recently issued, and at this date was just getting under way.

In pianos, organs, band instruments and general musical merchandise we had a large trade and carried a heavy stock. The two floors in the opera-house, 180 by 30 feet each, and as much room in the rear building, were filled to overflowing, beside the basement, in which was the type-setting and printing department. One can get some idea of the space required simply for a fair stock of books for such a trade as we had by considering how much room twenty-five cords of wood would take, and then, by figuring, ascertain that the ninety thousand " Triumph," spoken of above, would make more than twenty-five cords of books.

And now the memorable autumn of 1871 had come. Our presses had been at work all summer, and great piles of books filled the basement of the main building, ready for the fall trade. They would all be gone in a few weeks, so we did not take out a special insurance upon them, but assumed the

risk for that short time ourselves. I lived then in Groveland
Park, near the Chicago University, about four miles south
from our place of business. Between three and four o'clock
in the morning of the ninth of October some one waked me
and said Jerome Beardslee was at the door in a buggy and
wanted to see me. What could Jerome want at that time in
the morning, and why should he come in a buggy, since he
lives next door but one? I got up and tried to light the gas,
but there was none. I hurried on my clothes and went down.
"What is the matter, Jerome?" "There's a great fire down
town, and it is spreading fearfully. Our store is gone, but I
got the books out, and have just brought them home. I am
going back, and if you would like to ride with me you can.
I think you'll be in time to see your place go." I went, and
when we got within a mile of the fire we began to see signs
of the great disaster. Groups of men, women and children
(some scantily clad) were standing by such household goods
as they had brought to where they supposed they were out
of the reach of the flames. Team after team added to the
number until the streets were lined with the fugitives and
such of their belongings as they could save.

The wind blew fiercely from the south-west, so the flames
spread less rapidly our way, but on the north side nearly all
the people who thought their goods were out of danger had
to move again and again, and finally see them burn for the
want of means to get them out on to the prairie beyond
the farthest houses, four miles from the center. Some who
placed their goods on the lake shore where there was a beach,
not only had to see them burn, but had to get into the water
to save their lives. The heat of the fire, maddened by the
tornado it had caused, was beyond conception. I saw delicate looking tongues of flame shoot across an open space
twenty or thirty feet wide, and a marble building dissolve
under their touch as if it had been of sand. The action of a

gigantic compound blow-pipe was the only thing to which
one could liken those streams of flame and their effect.
Nothing could stand before them.   In the presence of miles
of such intense heat our firemen and their steam engines
were as impotent as children with toy watering-pots would
have been.   To get hose near enough at any point to be of
any use would be to see it curl and shrivel as if it had been
made of paper.   In fact, much of the fire apparatus was destroyed before it could be got out of the way.   No complete
idea of this scene can be had without keeping before the mind
the fierce wind, filled with keen cutting sand and cinders that
hurled great flaming brands for blocks over the yet unburnt
houses.   When the fire had done its work but few walls
were standing as landmarks.   We could not tell, in the business part of the city, where the streets were.   Localities that
two days before were as familiar to us as the rooms of our
own houses were now a strange, wild desolation.

I was in time to see the costly and elegant opera-house
go.   I could not get near enough to see the rear building in
which was my working-room and library.   I wondered if
my green box was safe.   The young men in the store had
laughed among themselves a good deal because I often said,
" If there's a fire, save that green box."   It was an old paper
affair, but it contained my daily work and all my unpub-
lished manuscripts.   We had built a large brick vault in the
cellar of the rear building, but a few months before, to make
a safe place for the plates of our now very large catalogue.
It was the duty of the porter to put the green box in the
vault with the other valuables at night.   He had not done
so at this time, and Mr. Murray's brother Robert, who slept
near, and was hastily looking about just before the fire
reached there, saw it, and remembering my injunction, saved
it.   All our important plates were in the vault, excepting
those of the " Song King " and the " Curriculum."   They

were in use at the printing office, and were destroyed. New plates of the " Song King " were immediately made in Cleveland, but I revised the " Curriculum," and its present form is the result.

One of the noticeable things at the opera-house, as the fire approached it, was the announcement that Theodore Thomas' " unrivaled orchestra " would give a concert there that evening. When the flames enveloped the beautiful building I thought of their fine instruments, some of which had been left there, and my mind also ran over a list of the familiar and valuable objects belonging to us that were then being offered up in that fearful holocaust—the costly counters, desks, and general fittings of oak and maple, the long lines of shelves of sheet music, the cords of books in the basement, the hundreds of elegant pianos and organs, fine violins, guitars and band instruments, the still greater number of accordeons, and other small instruments, strings, reeds, etc., the printing office and presses, and the fine room in which F. W., Mr. Murray and myself had done so much pleasant and successful work. In a few minutes all were gone. It was sad, but the calamity was so general and so overwhelming that individual losses seemed insignificant in comparison, even though they reached the sum of a quarter of a million, as ours did.

The days immediately following the fire were passed in anxious waiting to see if the vault and safes had protected our plates and account books. It was some days before they were cool enough to open ; when they were, their contents were found to be safe, though some of the papers were scorched. Every mail, too, brought business letters that had to be attended to. I think the first orders for goods were sent to Cleveland and Cincinnati to be filled, but it was not long before we had a large dwelling house on Michigan avenue fitted up and stocked, and business went on. The

nights at first were filled with anxious forebodings. The
city was in total darkness, and reports were rife that incen-
diaries were about and would set fires for pillage. So for
weeks a patrol was organized to keep watch all night, and in
this all had to take part. Then the generous letters began
to come. The event was unprecedented, and the feeling it
awoke in friend for friend, and in the whole world for the
city was also unprecedented; we were overwhelmed with
kindness ; but all that is too well known to need repetition
here. I will reprint from the *Song Messenger* but one after
the fire, the following:

" So the smoke clears away, and the sun shines again, and from
every side sympathy and aid pour in. Read this from good Mr. Curwen, the extensive publisher of the tonic-sol-fa system in England :

"LONDON, November 10, 1871.

" *Dear Mr. Root:* Our agent, at 8 Warwick Lane, says he knows
Chicago well, and that there can be no doubt that your fine premises
are burned. Even if you are fully insured this interruption of business must cause you heavy loss and much care. I am very sorry.

" Will you kindly accept the enclosed cheque for Twenty Pounds,
to be used for the help of your people or any other sufferers by the
fire? Kindly let them know that it is from one who has delighted in
your music and has spread it abroad in England.

" My sons and I wish to be kindly remembered to your two sons.

" Hoping to hear of your welfare, I am, dear Mr. Root, yours, with
cordial respect,   JOHN CURWEN."

The paper goes on to say: "The £20 realized $107.44,
and are now on their mission of blessing." It continues : " I
ought to say that my sons visited Mr. Curwen during their
late stay in Europe, and were delighted with the excellent
working of his system; and I may add that we are really
tonic-sol-faists in this country as to the matter of key relationship, the difference being in notation."

As soon as it could be brought about, our business plans
for the future were adjusted. We had lost all our stock, but
the plates and copyrights remained, and if I would give up

some unencumbered real estate that I had, Mr. Cady and my brother would, with the above and the insurance money they hoped to get, undertake to pay the debts in full and go on with the business.   I finally agreed to this proposition, and then two firms were formed.   The first consisted of my brother E. T., Mr. Cady, and Mr. William Lewis, the well-known violinist, who had been with us for some years in charge of the " imported goods " department.   They continued under the name of Root & Cady, and proposed to deal only in pianos, organs, and the merchandise of Mr. Lewis' department.   The other firm consisted of my two sons, my brother William and myself.   We took the name of Geo. F. Root & Sons, and started with the expectation of confining ourselves to sheet music, music books, and music publishing.   In this arrangement I need not say it was clearly understood that I was to be free to resume my professional life untrammeled by business cares.   My son F. W. also provided for himself much in the same way.   William and Charles were to manage the business, whatever it might be.

One of Root & Cady's first acts was to sell the book catalogue, plates and copyrights to John Church & Co., of Cincinnati, and the sheet music plates and copyrights to S. Brainard's Sons, Cleveland.   These sales realized a large sum—in the neighborhood of one hundred and thirty thousand dollars, if I remember rightly—but so many insurance companies failed that they did not get half their insurance, and when the hard times, which followed the fire, came on, could not meet the great liabilities they had assumed, and were obliged to close up.   With the assistance of a wealthy friend we purchased their stock.   They went through bankruptcy, and Mr. Cady left the city.   My brother E. T. and Mr. Lewis then started in again, under the firm name of Root & Lewis, and we (Geo. F. Root & Sons) formed a connection with John Church & Co., of Cincinnati.   The last named arrangement came about naturally, because this Cincinnati firm were now the owners and publishers of our former books, which were still successful, and they desired to continue the works of the same authors on their list.

From the re-adjustment after the fire I was in my old life again—the Normal in the summer, conventions at various times and in various places, and at my desk making books and songs the rest of the time. The Normal of 1872 was held during the vacation of the Chicago University, in their fine building overlooking Lake Michigan, with Carl Zerrahn, Robert Goldbeck, F. W. Root, P. P. Bliss, James Gill, O. Blackman, C. A. Havens, and others, as my co-workers. We had also at this session Miss Cornelia Walker, now at the head of one of the Normal schools of California, as teacher of the "art of teaching." The University had shortly before conferred upon me the degree of Doctor of Music, and I speak of it here to remark that in this country that title is only a matter of courtesy. No examinations are required before it is given, and therefore it does not necessarily imply high musical attainments on the part of the recipient. I know of but two or three American-made Doctors of Music that I think could pass the examination required for that degree in England, and I regret to say I am not one of them.

From an account in the *Song Messenger* of this Normal, the following item comes in properly :

" Another day toward the close of the session is memorable as bringing to our knowledge an event of deep and sad interest to us all. A telegram was brought which read:

"' Father died peacefully last night at ten o'clock.

HENRY MASON.' "

How subduing was the effect, and how spontaneous and unanimous was the passage of the following resolution :

"*Resolved*, That in the death of Dr. Lowell Mason we recognize the loss of one who in matters of church music and musical education in this country is the great reformer of the century."

All felt that as teachers, choir leaders or writers of people's music we owed a debt of eternal gratitude to the man whose long life and noble work and powerful influence had done so much to place the musical profession in the honorable position it occupies at the present time.

CHAPTER XIV.

1873–1886, CHICAGO — BUSINESS RE-ADJUSTMENTS — VARIOUS
NORMAL INSTITUTES AND CONVENTIONS—THE MEMORABLE
CENTENNIAL YEAR—PARK CHURCH AT ELMIRA—GRASSHOP-
PERS—A FURTHER LIST OF BOOKS—ENGLISH EDITIONS—
PASSAGE TAKEN TO CROSS THE WATER AGAIN.

AFTER the purchase of the stock of the old firm in 1873,
Geo. F. Root & Sons went on doing a general music
business, John Church & Co. and ourselves being the publishers of our works.   It was a time of great business de-
pression, but we had a "tower of strength" in the Cincinnati house, and Mr. Church's wise counsels guided us safely
through.   We still published the *Song Messenger*, and in its
list of those who then worked more or less with us are the
names of Palmer, Bliss, Straub, Matthews, Murray, Case,
McGranahan, Gill, Blackman and Whittemore.   Mr. Matthews, F. W. Root and myself were, in turn, editors of the
Messenger, but all connected with us reported in it in regard to what they were doing.

The Normal of '73 was also held in the Chicago University, with Faculty as in '72, excepting that Florence Zieg-
feld, the present head of the Chicago College of Music, was
the principal piano teacher, Louis Falk, organist, and Elias
Bogue, with F. W. Root, in voice teaching.   The Normal
of '74 was held in the U. P. College, in Monmouth, Ill.; F.
W. Root, Carl Wolfsohn and myself, principals; Bliss, Os-
car Mayo and Mrs. Cooley (model lessons), assistants.   The
Normal of '75 was in Somerset, Pa.; G. F. R., principal, C.
C. Case, James McGranahan, T. P. Ryder, Frank Walker.
C. C. Williams and myself, teachers.

In 1864 my home in Chicago was at the corner of Wabash avenue and Van Buren street.   I sold the place in '69. In '71 the fire swept it away.   In '72 some fine brick stores were built on the lot, one of which we occupied, but we did not stay there long.   When the old business center was rebuilt we went back near to where the opera-house formerly stood.   In '74 a second great fire visited Chicago. If the first had not been so vast, this one would have made some noise in the world, for it burned many acres of houses and stores, and destroyed millions of property.   It reached just far enough to take the building we had just left, and so the site of my former home was burned over for the second time.

In '74 important changes took place.   My son Charles sold his interest in our publications to John Church & Co., and went into other business, and the Root & Sons Music Co. was formed.   In '75 the firms of Root & Lewis and Chandler & Curtiss joined us.   John Church & Co. were the principal owners of the stock of the new company, and their abundant resources at once gave it standing and security.   At the suggestion of my brother, E. T. Root, Charles C. Curtiss was appointed manager.   I had been nominally free from business cares since the fire, but really had not been without some anxiety consequent upon starting again with so small a capital.   But now our interests were in safe and strong hands, and, to adapt Mr. Longfellow's famous lines to my case—the cares that had infested *my* day, folded their tents like the Arabs and as silently stole away, and I gave myself once more, with whole-hearted freedom, to my professional work.

All who had been connected with us as Normal students, and afterwards as teachers and authors, now looked to the Cincinnati house as publishing headquarters, and in '76 the *Song Messenger* was merged into *The Musical Visitor*, which from that time became our medium of communication with

the musical public. Ah, memorable '76! We went to the
great Centennial celebration in Philadelphia, and then to our
pleasant Normal in Towanda, Pa. ; Case, McGranahan, Ryder, Coffin, Williams, Bliss, F. W. Root and myself, teachers.
We then separated for our autumn and winter work.
Toward the close of the year our beloved Bliss and his wife
went down into that valley of fire and death at Ashtabula,
disappearing from the earth as completely as did Elijah in
his flaming chariot.   Not a shred or vestige of them or their
belongings was ever found.   Mr. Bliss' unselfish devotion to
his work made for him such friends while he lived and such
mourners when he died as few men have ever had.   It was
also in '76, at Christmas time, in Delaware, O., that the National Music Teachers' Association held its first session.   I
was glad to aid at the beginning of that important enterprise,
but have not participated since, as the subsequent meetings
have been in the summer when Normal or something else
demanded my attention.

Normal had now settled down into four weeks' sessions,
beginning always on the first Monday after the Fourth of
July.   In '77 it was held in Warren, O. ; in '78 in Richmond,
Ind. ; in '79 and '80 in Jamestown, on Chautauqua Lake,
New York ; in '81, Erie, Pa. ; in '82, Kittanning, Pa., and a
short term in Brookville, Pa. ; in '83 in Erie again, and a
short session in Eau Claire, Wis., and in '85 in Elmira, N. Y.

This Institution usually goes to a town because some
musical person in it, in whom the people have confidence,
represents its advantages to prominent citizens who bring
about the necessary offer of buildings and the guarantee of
a certain number of scholarships.   All other things being
equal, the coolest towns have the preference.   We delight
in being by Lake Michigan, or Erie, or lovely Chautauqua,
though Kittanning and Brookville, Pa., and Eau Claire,
Wis., were on pleasant rivers, which answered a good pur-

pose. Elmira, N. Y., could not offer much in the way of a river, but she could give us the most beautiful and convenient place for our work that we have ever had.

Picture to yourself a long stone structure on one side of a small park, with great trees in front and almost bending over it. At one end a large auditorium with a fine organ; in the center a Sunday-school room below, and a lecture and entertainment room above, each capable of seating four hundred persons, and at the other end the "church home," consisting of parlors, library, some lodging rooms, and all the conveniences of a well-ordered house, all connected and under one roof, and you have PARK CHURCH, the home of the Normal of '85. It must have been more than thirty years ago that Thomas K. Beecher, nearly the youngest member of that celebrated family, was settled over that society in Elmira. He gradually got his people to look to the day when a building should be reared which should contain not only a suitable audience room for Sunday worship, but rooms and conveniences for the enjoyment of the young people, and a home for the poor wayfarer who might need temporary shelter from poverty or evil influences. This was done, but not until all the money was raised or pledged to pay for it—one hundred and thirty-two thousand dollars. Mr. Beecher had constantly urged that there be no debt to be a drag upon them when their magnificent plan went into operation.

It was characteristic of pastor and people to say, as they did to us: "Your work is calculated to improve and help people. That is what this building is for. Use it during our church vacation. The whole of it is freely placed at your disposal." It was a delightful session—the perfection of the building for the various exercises of the class, the interest of the people as shown in the attendance upon recitals and concerts, and the assurance of a welcome if we would return, no one who was there will ever forget. We should have returned the next summer, but I went to England, of which visit I will speak later.

The general scope and work of the Institution may be seen in the subjoined daily program of one of the above named sessions :

MORNING.

Preliminary, from 8:15 to 8:55, *Intermediate Harmony Class.*

9:00. Opening Exercises (devotional), followed by G. F. Root's specialties—*Vocal Drill* and *Notation* for *Elementary Singing Classes.*

10:10. Recess.

10:20. *Voice Culture* in *Class*, Frederic W. Root.

11:05. Recess.

11:15. *Harmony* and *Composition*—in two classes. *Elementary*, G. F. Root; *Advanced*, F. W. Root.

AFTERNOON.

2:00. Clubs for the practice of conducting and of giving class lessons, called, respectively, the " Conducting Club " and the " Teachers' Club." Each member acts as conductor or teacher in turn, and is criticised at the close of his work.

3:00. *Sight Reading* and *Drill* in Anthems, Glees and Part-Songs.

3:50. Recess.

4:00. Monday and Wednesday, Emil Liebling's *Pianoforte Recitals*. Tuesday and Thursday, *Vocal Recitals*, bringing out the Soloists and Members of the Institute in individual performances.

4:45. Close.

EVENING.

7:45. Monday, Tuesday, Wednesday and Thursday evenings, CHORUS and ORATORIO practice, CARL ZERRAHN, conductor. Concerts every Friday evening, closing with " THE MESSIAH " on the 31st.

PROGRAMS OF PIANOFORTE RECITALS.

First Recital.

MONDAY, JULY 6TH, AT 4 P. M.

1. Andante, Op. 32 . . . . . . *Thalberg*
2. *a.* Solitude . . . . *Hoffman*
   b. Cricket Polka . . *L. De Meyer*
3. *a.* Barcarolle . . . . . *Rubinstein*
   b. Fantasie " Lucrezia Borgia "
   Bendel

Second Recital.

WEDNESDAY, JULY 8TH, AT 4 P. M.

1. *a.* Gavotte, B minor . . . . . *Bach*
   b. Andante, A major . . . . *Mozart*
   c. Perpetuum Mobile . . . . *Weber*
2. *a.* Menuet, A-flat . . . *Boccherini*
   b. Albumblatt, E minor . . . *Grieg*
   c. The Two Skylarks . *Leschetitzky*
3. *a.* Feu Follet . . . . *Liebling*
   b. Nocturne, Op. 17 . . . . *Brassin*
   c. Polonaise . . . . . . *Scharwenka*

Third Recital.

MONDAY, JULY 13TH, AT 4 P. M.

1. Recollections of Home . . . . *Mills*
2. *a.* Scherzino, Op. 18 . . *Moszkowski*
   b. Nocturne, A major . . . . *Field*
   c. Gavotte, E minor . . . . . *Silas*
3. *a.* Silver Spring . . . . . . *Bendel*
   b. La Cachoucha . . . . . . *Raff*

Fourth Recital.

WEDNESDAY, JULY 15TH, AT 4 P. M.

1. *a.* Sonata, G minor . . . . *Scarlatti*
   b. Prelude and Fugue, D major,
   Bach
2. Sonata Pathetique, Op. 13, *Beethoven*
3. *a.* Soirée de Vienne, No. 7 . . *Liszt*
   b. Nocturne, Op 9, No. 2 . . *Chopin*
   c. Gavotte Moderne . . . *Liebling*

Fifth Recital.

MONDAY, JULY 20TH, AT 4 P. M.

1. Rondo Capriccioso, Op. 14,
   Mendelssohn
2. *a.* Albumblatt . . . . . *Liebling*
   b. Le Tourbillon . . . . . *Goldbeck*
3. *a.* Valse Caprice, Op. 29 . . . *Mills*
   b. Melody in F . . . . . *Rubinstein*
   c. Polka Fantastique . . *Brandeis*

Sixth Recital.—Historical Program.

WEDNESDAY, JULY 22D, AT 4 P. M.

1. *a.* Sonata, A major, *Scarlatti*, 1683-1757.
   b. Prelude and Fugue, C minor, *Bach*, 1685-1750.
   c. Variations, E major, *Haendel*, 1684-1759.
   d. Turkish March, *Mozart*, 1756-1791.
2. Moonlight Sonata, *Beethoven*, 1770-1827.
3. *a.* Rondo Brillante, *Weber*, 1786-1826.
   b. Menuet, *Schubert*, 1797-1828.
   c. Songs Without Words, *Mendelssohn*, 1809-1847.
   d. Ende vom Lied, *Schumann*, 1810-1856.
4. *a.* Marche Funèbre, *Chopin*, 1809-1849.
   b. La Fileuse, *Raff*, 1822.
   c. Kammenoi-Ostrow, . *Rubinstein*, 1830.
   d. Polonaise, E major, *Liszt*, 1811.

Seventh Recital.

MONDAY, JULY 27TH, AT 4 P. M.

1. *a.* Impromptu, Op. 29,
   b. Étude, Op. 10, No. 5,
   c. Mazurka, Op. 33, No. 4,
   d. Valse, Op. 34, No. 1,
2. *a.* Nocturne, Op. 37, No. 2,
   b. Scherzo, Op. 31,
3. *a.* Berceuse. Op. 57,
   b. Polonaise, Op. 53, *Chopin*

Eighth Recital.

WEDNESDAY, JULY 29TH, AT 4 P. M.

1. G minor Fugue . . . . . *Bach-Liszt*
2. *a.* Flashes from the West, *Goldbeck*
   b. Silver Spring . . . . . *Mason*
   c. Hungarian Melody . . . . *Liszt*
3. *a.* Romanza, Op. 5 . . *Tschaikowsky*
   b. Marche Héroique . . *Saint-Saens*

In looking over the list of Musical Associations that I have conducted since the fire, I find it too long even to mention. As I glance at the list, however, my eye catches the line: "Centennial celebration of the settlement of Sheffield, Mass., June 19, '76." This is my native town, and

the musical exercises there were of peculiar interest to the
people who knew my parents, and to myself on their account.   I was a small boy when we moved to North Reading, but I remembered well the beautiful Berkshire mountains that looked so near and were so far, the lovely Housa-
tonic which flows through the valley, and the wide street
and magnificent elms of the dear old village which I am
proud to claim as my birthplace.   Among the kinfolk that
welcomed me on this occasion was Dr. Orville Dewey, one
of America's eminent divines, who was there also at his
birthplace.   That brings to my mind that Dr. Dewey and
Wm. Cullen Bryant, who was also a native of Berkshire
County, were both school-mates of my father, and a few
years before, while I was engaged in some musical work in
Great Barrington (the next town), Mr. Bryant was there,
and I had the pleasure of a few kind words from him in
remembrance of his old school-fellow.

   As I look along the list, the word "grasshoppers"
catches my eye and brings to mind a wagon ride from a
convention in Clarinda, Ia., to another at College Springs,
fifteen miles distant, and a description that the driver gave
me of the ravages of those terrible pests.   During the convention I was introduced to one of the large farmers who
had suffered by them, and was greatly interested in his
graphic description of what had befallen him : " We had had
two years of light crops," he began, " and I needed some
good wheat and a lot of it the worst way, so I put in six
hundred acres, and you never saw anything so fine as that
was when it was about half grown.   I was happy !   That
crop was going to fix me all right.   Well, I drove in here
to church one Sunday morning—I live about four miles out
—and when I got back there wasn't a spear of my wheat
standing ; the ground where it stood was as black as if it had
been burnt over, and the 'hoppers had traveled on."   " But

you lived through it," I said. " Oh, yes," he answered, " I'm all right now."

In '81 Mr. E. V. Church, Mr. John Church's nephew, took the management of the business, Mr. Curtiss having left for a trip to Europe. Mr. Lewis had already made other business arrangements, and now my brother, E. T., sold his stock in the company to go into business with his sons. The arrangements thus described remain to the present time, with the exception that John Church & Co. became tired of the inconvenience of occupying stores owned by other people, and bought the white marble building at the corner of Wabash avenue and Adams street, which fine premises we occupy now.

My books, after the fire and up to my second trip abroad in '86, were: " The New Curriculum," " The Glory," " The Hour of Praise," " The Guide to the Pianoforte," " The Cabinet Organ Companion," " The Normal Musical Hand-Book," " The New Song Era " (with my son F. W.), " The Choir and Congregation," " The Männerchor," " The Trumpet of Reform," " The Model Organ Method," " The Palace of Song," " The Realm of Song," " The Chorus Castle," " The Teachers' Club," " The Organist at Home," " First Years in Song Land," " Our Song World " (with C. C. Case), " Pure Delight " and " Wondrous Love " (also with Mr. Case), and the following cantatas: In the first one, " The Song Tournament," I was assisted in preparing the libretto by Palmer Hartsough, one of our Normals, who has great ingenuity in adapting words to music, and then I made the valued acquaintance of Hezekiah Butterworth, of Boston, the well-known author and poet, who prepared the librettos to " Under the Palms," " Catching Kriss Kringle," " David, the Shepherd Boy," " The Name Ineffable," " The Choicest Gift," and " Faith Triumphant." Then followed " Flower Praise " and " Santa Claus' Mistake," with librettos by my

daughter, Clara Louise Burnham. Of the Sunday-school
and Gospel songs, not before mentioned, the following are
best known : " Why do you wait, dear brother? " " Jewels,"
" Ring the bells of heaven," " Knocking, knocking, who is
there? ' " Along the river of time," " Where are the reap-
ers? " " We are watching, we are waiting," " The beacon
light," " Because He loved me so," " Altogether lovely,"
" Never give up the right way," and " Behold, the Bride-
groom cometh."

    " Under the Palms " was the first cantata to unite adults
and children (the choir and Sunday-school) in a connected
performance, and its success was immediate. Not long
after its publication in 1880 I received a letter from the
London Sunday-school Union, saying that they had issued
that work, and that it was being extensively sung throughout the kingdom. The letter enclosed a gratuity in the
shape of an English bank-note, and further said if I would
write them another cantata of the same kind they would pay
a regular royalty on it. " The Choicest Gift " was the result of that request, but in the meantime the firm of John
Curwen & Sons (consisting now only of the sons, the father
being dead) wrote me that I should soon receive an English
copy of " David, the Shepherd Boy,"and that they proposed
to pay a voluntary royalty on all copies of it that they sold.
This was a purely friendly and generous act on their part,
as all American compositions were as free to them as theirs
are to us. They issued it in both notations, and an excellent English musician added a harmonium accompaniment,
which is printed in a separate book. They also had it arranged for a large orchestra.

    About this time I received a letter from Messrs. Bailey
& Ferguson, of Glasgow, Scotland, to know if I would write
a cantata for them. My publishers soon arranged the matter, and " Faith Triumphant " was the result. An arrange-

ment was made to furnish the Glasgow house a set of plates by duplicating them as the book went through the press in Cincinnati.

I had long desired to go to England once more, and it now occurred to me that it would be pleasant to get to Glasgow soon after my cantata, and perhaps do something in the way of helping it start in Scotland. So when I found my publishers thought it a good plan I decided to go. After I had secured my passage I received a third letter from the London Sunday-school Union about a third cantata for them, to which I replied that I would call in a few days and talk it over.

CHAPTER XV.

ON BOARD THE STEAMSHIP ETHIOPIA—GLASGOW—FIRST SUN-
DAY IN LONDON — ST. MARTIN'S-IN-THE-FIELDS — INTER-
LUDES — THE LONDON SUNDAY-SCHOOL UNION—THE CUR-
WENS — VOLUNTARY ROYALTIES — HERNE HOUSE — MR.
EVANS AND THE LONDON PUBLIC SCHOOLS.

ON July 17, 1886, I found myself on board the steamship
Ethiopia, of the Anchor Line, bound for Glasgow, Scotland.

It is interesting to observe the change that comes over
some people at the beginning of a sea-voyage, as the billows,
which at first seem to them so grand or so graceful, gradually become objects of utter aversion and disgust—but I will
not enlarge. It is sufficient to say that in our case on the
fourth day out two-thirds of the sick ones were back to their
rations, and we had an excellent voyage.

We had a good deal of music as we steamed along, there
being there a piano and organ, and several good players and
singers among the passengers. One evening the program
was varied by a mock trial. A nice old gentleman of decidedly patriarchal appearance, who had paid a good deal of
attention to the ladies, "without distinction of age or previous condition of servitude," as the indictment read, was
accused of being a Mormon elder, seeking proselytes. Being
conducted in good taste by real lawyers, the trial afforded
much entertainment. The jury was composed entirely of
ladies, who rendered a unanimous verdict in the prisoner's
favor.

Sunday divine service was conducted by a clergyman

from Toronto. There is an opening from the main cabin to the room above called the music-room, in which is an excellent organ and a good piano. The choir, composed of a few of the best singers among the passengers, was up there, and the effect was good, the only trouble being that the player had to be guarded lest the rolling of the ship should send him off his seat.

On Sunday evening at twilight the organist began playing quietly some of the older tunes, gradually coming nearer those of modern times. The passengers gathered round, and when he got to " Nearer, my God, to Thee " and " The Shining Shore," began to join in. This led to one of the most genuine Sunday night sings that I have ever heard. One after another called for his or her favorite, until about all the well-known tunes and gospel songs had been sung. The roar of the winds and dash of the waves outside mingling with our music would have perhaps carried our thoughts back to the Pilgrims' " Songs on the Sea," but for the beat of the engine and the knowledge that the Pilgrim fathers would not have given our gospel songs a place in their stern devotions.

The last day of our voyage. All day along the northern coast of Ireland. " Emerald " is the word, as we look on the beautiful fields and hills, and here comes the Giant's Causeway. " Don't you see the giant? " says an old sailor. " No," I answer. " Why, there, leaning his arm on the rock, so, and his feet down in the water." I couldn't see him, but all could see the wonderful pillar-like structure stretching along for miles like gigantic organ pipes.

And now up the Clyde. Fields, lawns, forests, hills, towns, country seats, castles, and then ship-yards as we near Glasgow, where the great iron steamers and ships of the world are made. Such a clang and clatter as the thousands of hammers rang out upon the iron ribs and plates as we passed!

Glasgow at last. To the hotel and then to Messrs. Bayley & Ferguson's to see if the plates of the new cantata had come. As they had not yet arrived I went back to the hotel and waited until Mr. Bayley should have leisure to show me about the town.

Glasgow is emphatically a stone city. Not a wooden structure in it, and I think Mr. Bayley said there was none of brick—at any rate, I saw none. I was not prepared to find Glasgow the second city in the empire, but so it is.

We went at evening to a park just out of the city, to hear a band play—a beautiful place of hills and valleys, fine trees and flowers. "Here," said Mr. Bayley, "where the band are now playing, was fought the battle that lost Queen Mary her kingdom. She watched it from the hill over there (a half mile or so off), and when she saw the day was against her, fled, and was never again seen in Scotland."

Many such things of historic interest came up, but I will not inflict guide-book talk upon my readers. It is sufficient to say that I passed a memorable and most pleasant day with our Glasgow publisher—a long one, too, light as day at nine o'clock at night, with twilight until ten or after.

As the plates of the cantata were delayed I did not wait, but took the " Midland " to London the next day. Tremendous speed, but so smooth that one could read or write without difficulty. I fell into conversation with an intense Englishman, who had been in our country, and who was loud in his preference for everything English. Speaking of the compartment in which we were locked, he said: " Now, if there is anybody on the train that I don't want to see, he can't get in here." I did *not* answer, " If there is anybody in here that I don't want to see, I can't get out," but I thought it.

I enjoyed some nice children that were in the compartment, and at one of the stations bought a basket of strawberries for distribution. It was a good sized basket, and, noticing that the bottom of the basket was not half way up to lessen its size, I said to myself, "How much more honest they are over here in these matters," but some cabbage leaves at the bottom of the basket threw some doubt on the superior honesty of these neighbors across the water.

My first Sunday in London I attended Argyle-square Church in the morning and "St. Martin's-in-the-fields" in the evening. Fine organs and fine organists. Excellent singers. In "St. Martin's" a surpliced choir of men and boys in the chancel, and admirable music. The hymn tunes ecclesiastical, but sung in quick time, so nothing heavy about them. All this, to say that in the five hymns heard in the morning and evening, *there was not one interlude*. There certainly was no more need of interludes in those hymns than there would have been in the chants, which were so freely sung. How inspiriting they were! The glow that commenced at the beginning of the hymn did not die out at the end of each verse, but increased steadily to the end of the song.

In this connection I may mention that I was in Lancashire for a few days soon after my arrival in England, and on the occasion of a religious gathering heard some hymns sung by a congregation of perhaps six hundred people. The tunes were modern English ("Barnby," "Smart," etc.), excellent in every way, and sung heartily and well. Fine, strong voices the Lancashire people have—the high tones good and in tune. But what struck me especially there, also, was that *not one interlude* was played during the evening. I was a good deal interested in the remark of a friend there, who said: "To use an Americanism, interludes are 'played out'—they are only used occasionally to lengthen the hymn during a collection." I am sure if our people could once hear how a hymn of five or six long verses, with a good tune, can go through, not only without weariness but with positive satisfaction, they would not put up with the *interruptions*, or worse, of interludes.

How they hold on to old names over there! I suppose St. Martin's *was* in the "fields," but there isn't a field within miles of it now. It is in the very heart of London. In its old neighbor, Westminster Abbey, I was much attracted by the new marble bust of Longfellow, especially as some admirer had placed a delicate bunch of flowers in the folds of the marble, making a sort of button-hole bouquet. Its contrast to the blackened and grim surroundings was striking. But to return to musical matters.

The London Sunday-school Union publish "Under the Palms" and "The Choicest Gift." The week before I left home I received a letter from them, saying they would like another cantata of that grade. I called upon them and arranged for future publications. My readers doubtless know that the English people have been using our American music for many years. All Foster's songs, and, in fact, pretty much all the music of a simple and medium grade that has been popular in America, have had a corresponding popularity in England. The first American cantata printed in England was "The Flower Queen." Since then nearly, if not quite, all our cantatas have appeared there, soon after their issue in America, proving not that we are better composers than the English, but that we are nearer and more in sympathy with those for whom we write. I think I do not violate any principle of propriety if I say that a high official in the Sunday-school Union added that the American cantatas that they had published had in their music a "go" (to use his expression) that they did not find elsewhere. This induces the Union to offer a royalty for what they want, although there is no international copyright.

I had word from Messrs. Bayley & Ferguson, of Glasgow,

at this time, that the plates of " Faith Triumphant" had arrived, and that the work would be issued promptly in the
standard and tonic-sol-fa notations.

Years ago, when Rev. John Curwen was commencing the
tonic-sol-fa enterprise he used a great deal of our American
singing-school music, which is free there, there being no
international copyright law.   After he passed away his sons
continued publishing from American works such music as
suited their purpose, but since the tonic-sol-fa movement has
grown stronger, and its adherents have made higher attainments, it is not the simpler music they take so much as the
cantatas—that is, so far as I am concerned.   These, beginning with " The Flower Queen " and ending with " Florens,
the Pilgrim "—fourteen in all—are printed by them in the
staff notation as well as in " tonic-sol-fa."

I say all this to explain why I, who neither teach nor
write in tonic-sol-fa, was the recipient of such unbounded
kindness from those friends, especially from Mr. J. Spencer
Curwen, the present head of the movement, at whose home
I stayed.   The father made a substantial recognition of what
he was pleased to consider his obligations to us at the time
of the Chicago fire, as I have previously mentioned, and the
present firm of their own accord proposed the royalty on
" David, the Shepherd Boy," of which I have spoken.

Explaining thus how it happened that I was a guest at
" Herne house," Mr. Curwen's residence, and to some extent
why Mr. Curwen took so much trouble to help me to hear
the representative music of the English people, I will state
briefly what we did.   Of course it was results that I sought
—to know how the people sang as compared with ourselves,
and how the reading and understanding of music compared
with the same things on our side, as Mr. Evans, the superintendent of music in the public schools of London (1,100
schools, 300,000 children), told me the first time I met him:

"I say to the teachers, take what method you please; I shall report you according to *results*. If they are good we have no fault to find with the method." This, of course, is eminently just. Let the teacher do his work in his own way; simply hold him responsible for results. (As a matter of fact, a large majority of the London schools have adopted tonic-sol-fa.)

In this spirit I tried to listen to such singing as I had an opportunity to hear in England. First the voices, how they were used, then the words and expression, then the reading and comprehension of principles (where I could ascertain about the latter things).

CHAPTER XVI.

THE WORK OF THE TONIC-SOL-FA COLLEGE — MR. BEHNKE'S
LIGHT TO THE THROAT—ENGLAND AND DICKENS — THE
BOYS OF THE MEDWAY UNION—DON—THE STAFFORDSHIRE
POTTERIES AND THE BURSLEM SINGERS—EPPING FOREST
AND THE LAWN PARTY AT FOREST GATE—REV. JOHN CUR-
WEN'S GRAVE—THE CHOIR OF THE CHAPEL ROYAL—MR. J.
A. BIRCH AND "THE HAYMAKERS."

THE Normal term at the Tonic-sol-fa College was near
its close when I arrived in London. It was like being
at home to be there, for they have our plans for their work
—teaching class, voice class, harmony class, etc., but with
some improvements not dependent upon tonic-sol-fa notation which we might well adopt. The first work that I
heard was Mr. McNaught's—teaching the students to teach
children. For this purpose a class of children from a neighboring school was brought in, and *real work* was done, the
students trying their hand at it after the model was given.
We have sometimes had juvenile classes at our Normals, but
not just in this way. Capital teacher, Mr. McNaught. Criticisms keen and incisive, but given with such vivacity, and
at the same time with such evident kindliness and desire for
the students' welfare, that the severest comments were received not only without mortification but with evident enjoyment. Normal workers know well the great importance
of such an ability.

Next, Mr. Proudman's voice class. Admirable work. Mr.
Proudman will be remembered as the conductor who took
to Paris the English choir, which created such enthusiasm

in an international competition a few years ago. There were
some new points in Mr. Proudman's work which seemed to
me very important and useful.

The harmony work by Mr. Oakey and Mr. McNaught
interested me much. Some exercises in the way of noting
harmonies as they were heard were especially good. The
idea and value of "ear harmony" as distinguished from
"eye harmony" they fully understand in this institution.

I had been much interested for two or three years in
reading of the investigations and researches of Mr. Emil
Behnke in matters pertaining to the voice, so it was with
much pleasure that I found he was to lecture here, and that
I could hear him. When I was introduced he said: "Ah!
I have read your articles on the voice with great pleasure.
They abound in good sense and valuable ideas." I had to
say that the articles were not written by myself, but by my
son, F. W. Root (but I dare say there was some pride in the
emphasis with which I uttered the words "my son").

Think of applying an electric light of thirty thousand
candle power to the throat to see what is going on inside!
But let me repeat how he explained the experiment as well
as I can remember it. He began by saying: "Hold your
open hand close to a strong light and you can see something
of the light through where the fingers join together; or hold
a light behind the ear and the same transparency may be
observed. So I thought a very powerful light might be so
brought to bear upon the outside of the throat that the vocal
cords inside would get light enough to be reflected in a mir-
ror, and in that way reveal their different positions for the
different registers of the voice. I applied to Sir Wm. Sie-
mens (a distinguished electrician of London) for the use of
apparatus to try my experiment. This was kindly granted,
and I arranged the light in a box with a tube to the throat
which concentrated and directed the light to the point to be

THE STORY OF A MUSICAL LIFE.   179

investigated." Without going further into particulars, I will only say his experiment was successful, and he showed photographs of the vocal cords in various positions caused by different pitches of the voice.

They do know how to treat boys' voices in England, at least the teachers whose work I have seen, do. But I ought to say that Mr. Curwen, sparing no trouble nor expense, arranged for me to hear the best. Our first trip was to Chatham and Rochester, which practically form one town, being on either side of the river Medway, about forty miles from London. The first thought on arriving there was of one of Mr. Pickwick's early adventures. It is surprising how strong a hold Dickens' stories have upon the American mind. I found I was not alone in thinking of Dickens the first thing when I came across a name, or place, or scene that he has mentioned or described. We might almost say that it is not so much that Dickens describes England as that England illustrates Dickens. There were the ruins of Rochester Castle, "the lonely field near Fort Pitt" where Mr. Winkle and Lieut. Tappleton met for the duel which did not take place, and the bridge where "dismal Jemmy" so excited Mr. Pickwick's sympathies in the early morning. We saw them all, though the gentleman who pointed them out knew little or nothing of Dickens.

But to continue my subject:—We went to see and hear the boys of the "Medway Union." You would hardly suppose that that means a work-house, but such is the fact. It is a large establishment, with people of all ages in it. The children are, of course, of the lowest grade, many of them the veriest waifs of community, but they have excellent school privileges, and the head master, Mr. James A. Price, fortunately for them, not only loves music, but understands it and knows how to teach it as very few professional teachers do. Indeed, to his rare skill the extraordinary results that

we listened to are due.   What did it matter how they expressed or noted what they sang?   It was, in point of fact,
a tonic-sol-fa choir, but I did not think about that at all at
first.   It was the *singing* that struck me and delighted me
as no boys' singing up to that time had ever done.   There
were about forty of the little fellows in the choir, carrying
three well-balanced parts—the sopranos beautifully sweet
and clear, and the altos of admirable quality—not a harsh
voice in the whole number, nor one chest-tone forced beyond its proper place.   They sang without accompaniment,
but there was no flatting nor singing out of tune in any way.

They sang one or two songs of German origin, if I remember rightly, at first, and then four or five of mine.   It
is the same everywhere here.   Wherever the tonic-sol-faists
have worked, American music has found a use and a home.
Mine would naturally be sung where I went, as a complimentary attention.

After the singing Mr. Price had a few of the boys play
violins and violas while he played the 'cello, and after that a
large drum and fife corps, also composed of the choir boys,
performed admirably;   only, as it was damp weather, the
performance was in a room and the din almost deafening.   I
must not omit to mention a very prominent member of this
happy company—for happy it is, as the beaming faces of the
little fellows abundantly testify.   This individual is " Don,"
a monstrous dog of the St. Bernard persuasion.   Wherever
the boys are, there is Don.   Whenever they assemble for
singing he brings up the rear and stretches his huge bulk in
the aisle as near to them as he can get.   During the stun-
ning fife and drum performance, which would have set wild
any other dog I ever knew, Don walked around among the
instruments and players, placidly waving his great plume of
a tail, the picture of contentment and benevolence.   And
after the music, out in the paved court where some little

boys were at play, I shall never forget the affection manifested on both sides—how the little chaps clung to the great fellow, and how he seemed to feel the care of the entire group.

It will be a great pleasure always to call to mind the friends and events of that day : Mr. and Mrs. Price, and her mother (who has been the matron of the institution for many years), and the assistant teachers, and their noble work. The difference for good that in all probability they will have caused in the lives of those children can not be estimated by any earthly standard.

I now come to another most interesting event connected with my English visit. It was a journey to Burslem, in Staffordshire, by the kind arrangement of Mr. Curwen, and, as his guest, to hear one of the most celebrated choirs in the kingdom. Staffordshire is the great pottery county of England. It was in Burslem that Wedgewood lived and died. Wedgewood Hall, a beautiful building, is there erected to his memory, in which are wonders of the art which has made his name celebrated the world over. The choir is composed almost entirely of men, women and children who work in the potteries or are connected with that industry. On the way Mr. Curwen said: "I do not know whether there is something especially favorable to singing in their occupation, but it is certain that they have exceptionally good voices."

We were met at the station by Mr. Thomas Hulme, a prominent citizen and former mayor of the city, who took us to his fine residence on a commanding eminence in the suburbs. From there we went at seven to the Town Hall, where the performance was to take place. The hall which would hold a thousand or more people was packed on our arrival. On either side and in front of a good-sized organ were raised seats for the choir, already there, one hundred and seventy strong. The fact that this choir had sung my music a good deal in former years, and that the papers had announced our coming—Mr. Curwen's and mine—in a very kind and appreciative way, caused a hearty greeting on the part of both choir and audience as we entered.

I ought to say that this was a kind of public rehearsal of music to be performed at a competition of choral societies (they call them "choirs" in England) to take place at Liverpool the following week. The great competition piece was a double chorus by Bach, called "Be not afraid"—twenty-seven pages long in the Novello edition, and taking exactly ten minutes in performance. When I say that it is in eight parts, filled with the peculiar intricacies and difficulties of this great composer's music, and that it was sung magnificently *without notes and without accompaniment*, I think my readers will agree with me that it was a remarkable performance, well worth a long journey to hear. Mr. Curwen's remark about the voices was fully justified. They were not only beautiful in quality but of great power. Indeed, when the chorus began, the burst was so grand that I could hardly realize that only one-half the choir were singing.

There were other highly interesting performances during the evening, among which was a part-song by Pinsuti, most delicately sung; but I will not further particularize; yes, I must mention a test that Mr. Curwen, by request, gave to show the musical knowledge of the younger members of the choir. Two blackboards were brought on to the platform and two children called up to write what Mr. Docksey, the conductor, sang, he using the syllable *la*. The music in two parts had been prepared by Mr. Curwen before entering the hall, and was, of course, entirely unknown to the choir. The work was promptly and correctly done in the tonic-sol-fa notation, and then six other children—three on a part—were called up to sing what had been written, which was easily and well done, much to the delight of the audience. I presume they could have used the staff notation, but this was shorter.

I shall not soon forget the Burslem choir and its able conductor, and the pleasure that evening gave me.

Who has not read of that bold outlaw, Robin Hood, and his adventures in Epping Forest, then far away from London, but now near by? The forest did not go to London, but London came to the forest, the eight or nine miles out to "Forest Gate," where Mr. Curwen lives, being now a continuous city, a most pleasant and safe ride, the railway going sometimes over the streets and houses and other railways, sometimes under them, but never on their level. No "crossings," with flagmen whose best efforts can not prevent accidents, and no delays—everything like clock-work; a consummation devoutly to be wished for on our side of the water.

But I started to tell about a party—a lawn party on the borders of Epping Forest. An English lawn is something to see—the thick, soft grass, so level and green, is like cut velvet, and for bowls, ten-pins, croquet, and other outdoor games as good as a floor. The lawn at Mr. Curwen's place is of this kind, and is rendered more picturesque by being thickly bordered on the sides by fine trees, some old enough, perhaps, to have sheltered the bold outlaw and his merry men. Here the students of the sol-fa college, with the teachers and their ladies, assembled one lovely afternoon near the close of their term.

Right here let me say that if any one has an impression that these tonic-sol-fa people and their accomplished teachers do not know the staff notation, they are wonderfully mistaken. I only wish our people knew it as well. Why, the Curwen house prints everything it issues in the staff notation as well as in tonic-sol-fa. It is a curious fact that at first the other houses, Novello's, for instance, printed no tonic-sol-fa and the Curwens printed no staff. Now the Curwens print staff and Novello a great deal of tonic-sol-fa music. I am quite sure I am right in saying that all sol-fa-ists look forward to a knowledge of the staff notation as their crowning acquirement.

Somehow or other the impression has been extensively created in America that "Sol-fa" was to sweep all other no-tations out of existence. I don't know who did it—Mr. Seward says he didn't; but I do know that that is not the way the matter is regarded in England, and it is much to be regretted that there should be any misunderstanding about it, for the usefulness of the work as done there can not be denied, and the teaching that has grown with it that may be applied to the staff notation is of a very superior order.

The afternoon was delightful; groups playing games, others chatting, two long tables decked with flowers, near the trees, for supper, or, I should say, tea. They do nothing there without a cup of tea. At almost any kind of meeting having at all the social element in it the first thing is a cup of tea—a discussion, a speech meeting, a singing meeting. They don't seem to get on with any of them without first getting inspiration from the cup which "cheers," etc. I do not wonder, though, that it is so popular a beverage there. It is quite another thing from the article we know as tea. "Tea meetings" would never thrive on the kind we gener-ally get on our side of the water.

After tea a photographer appeared on the scene and placed the assembled company in a group, with the fine old "ivy-mantled" house for a background. "Come, doctor," they called. I was talking with some one a little way off. "You don't want me," I answered; "I'm not in the charmed circle." "But your music is, and we must have you." So there I am, in the excellent picture then taken.

I had the pleasure of meeting here Mr. Spedding Curwen,

the other member of the firm of J. Curwen & Sons, and its business manager, whose fine residence is not far away. Nothing could be more complete than the combination of these two men for the success of their important business enterprises; nor more delightful than the intercourse of their two families for the enjoyment of their home life.

After the picture, singing. There were too few lady students to have a mixed choir, but the men's choir, under the leadership of Mr. McNaught, was admirable. Mr. Proudman's voice work showed its rare excellence, especially in the upper tenors. Their tones were of beautiful quality, easily produced and true to pitch. Then Mr. Kestin, the teacher of elocution, gave some recitations. I wish some of our howling ranters could have heard him. The quiet sincerity with which he made every character his own, made me think of the answer a country friend once gave when asked how he liked Jefferson's acting in "Rip Van Winkle." "Why, I didn't see any *acting*. I saw a shif'less Dutchman that got druv off into the mountains, but he was such a good-natur'd feller I liked him fust rate." So Mr. Kestin was for the time whatever he assumed to be, carrying us all with him, in the same way. The drawing-room being on a level with the lawn, with windows opening out upon it, all could enjoy the solos—instrumental and vocal—with which the afternoon closed.

In connection with the romantic interest I felt in Epping Forest, a deep impression was made upon my mind about this time by a visit to Rev. John Curwen's grave. It is nearer what was the forest center, in a spot selected, I think his son said, by himself. A fine shaft bears an appropriate inscription, but his great monument is the reverence in which his memory is held by hundreds of thousands who have been the better for his modest and unselfish work.

My kind host knowing my desire to hear the representative music of England as far as possible, suggested, on a Sunday soon after, that we go to the Chapel Royal, St. James Palace, the worshiping place of royalty and nobility when in London.   Arriving in due time we were ushered by a solemn functionary—I forget his title—into some seats that we might occupy.   It is a small chapel, long and narrow, but rich and elaborate in decorations, particularly the part devoted to the royal family—but I won't go into guide-book talk. The first curious thing was the dress of the choir boys before they donned their white surplices (we saw them about the corridors of the palace).   It was of red and gold, very elaborate and costly, more military than religious-looking, but a distinguishing uniform that they must wear all the time. But the little fellows can sing!   Nothing but the severest of the English ecclesiastical music allowed—extremely difficult in all respects, and I should say only made tolerable to untrained ears by the beauty of the voices and the ease with which all difficulties were overcome.   The alto was sung by men.   We were invited to dinner by Mr. J. A. Birch, an acquaintance of Mr. Curwen, whose speaking voice indicates a fine, resonant base, but who is one of the altos, not only of this choir but of that of St. Paul's Cathedral, the services being at different hours.   I need not say that these positions mean exceptional gifts and attainments on the part of those who hold them.   The men of this particular choir are called "gentlemen of the chapel royal."   Mr. Birch is a highly successful conductor and teacher in London, and gratified me much by his hearty greeting.   In the course of conversation he said: " I have given your cantatas a great deal for many years; indeed, one of them has been more remunerative than any other work of the kind that I have ever had to do with—I mean ' The Haymakers.'   I have given it seventeen times."

On coming out of service we were just in time to see the

change of the Queen's guard in the court-yard of the palace, and to hear two numbers from one of the two best bands in the kingdom.   A Thomas orchestra performance was the only thing I could liken it to for finish and elegance.

CHAPTER XVII.

THE PARISH CHURCH—TRADITIONAL CHANTING—THE "SWAN-
LEY BOYS"—THE HALL OF PARLIAMENT—A RECEPTION ON
MR. CURWEN'S LAWN—FORTY CONDUCTORS—THE BRITISH
MUSEUM—A MUSICAL CATALOGUE—ONE OF THE LONDON
"CHOIRS"—THE SOUTH LONDON CHORAL INSTITUTE—DR.
ALLON'S CHURCH AT ISLINGTON—MY SIXTY-SIXTH BIRTH-
DAY—THE CRYSTAL PALACE AND "AUTUMN WINDS"—THE
CONCERT ON THE "CITY OF ROME."

GOING to "church" in England means but one thing—
the Church of England. Going to other religious
gatherings is called going to "chapel," or something of that
kind. One Sunday morning my kind host said, "Let us go
to the parish church to-day; the music will interest you."
It was a walk of perhaps a mile and a half from Forest Gate,
but when we got there it was indeed the parish church of
old England as immortalized in descriptions innumerable:
low, gothic, massive, ivy-clad, the old, gray tower rising
like the chief monument of the church-yard in which it is
placed. Groups of grown people and children, wending
their way among the grave-stones, realized in every particular the picture so familiar to us all of this peculiarly English
scene.

We entered at a side door, stepping upon the uneven
stone floor that had been worn by the footsteps of many
generations. The surpliced organist, in full sight, had just
commenced his voluntary. Soon the ministers and choir
of surpliced men and boys filed in, and service commenced.
I will not go into particulars, but would simply speak of the

excellent choir-singing there, as I have had occasion to do
of all the surpliced choirs I heard while in England, and of
the fine tunes and hearty singing of the congregation, in *all*
the hymns.   I did not hear one by choir alone, and *not an
interlude* during the entire time.

I think my readers will bear witness that I have not
sought the adverse side in my descriptions, but I must say
that chanting there, judged by every consideration excepting
tradition, is poor—more than that, it is to me irreverent.   I
will not judge others, but how any one who thinks the
words of the Bible should be read or intoned deliberately,
can be devotionally impressed by the unseemly haste and
inevitable confusion that this mode of chanting compels, I
do not understand.   And it is passing strange, that while
the "chapels," and dissenters generally, who have broken
off from the Church of England, repudiate mostly the modes
of that church, they stick to this race-horse chanting—that
is, so far as I have heard them.   The power of tradition is
astonishing.   It still holds sway over the Episcopal churches
of our country, but we have reason to be thankful that Dr.
Lowell Mason, a half a century ago, inaugurated the better
mode that prevails in our other churches; that is, the chants
so arranged that the words are uttered about as fast as the
reverent reader reads.

On the Monday following we went to the Swanley Or-
phan's Home, one of those noble institutions for the care and
training of children of which there are several about London.   This place is about twenty miles out, if I remember
rightly, delightfully situated on a breezy hill, and is remarkable for its boy choir, known as the "Swanley Boys."
I wish you could see the photograph before me—two hundred or more of these little fellows—taken in the Institution
(they teach the boys there all sorts of useful occupations);
a ruddier, happier set of little faces it would be hard to find.

I say "remarkable for its boy choir." I ought to say it is remarkable for its excellence in everything that relates to the welfare of the boys, but I will confine myself to the one thing that we went especially to observe.

The whole number sang first in two parts—just soprano and alto—but such music! I am sorry I did not take a note of what was done first—I think something by Mendelssohn, but what was most prominent was the Hallelujah chorus! As music, without tenor and base, it was of course lacking, but as a performance showing the musical attainments of the boys, and especially the masterly training of their voices, it was a great success. Every time the sopranos approached the high places that every conductor so much dreads, I thought " now they can not keep up that perfect pitch and sweetness," but they did, and when the sopranos gave the high A at "And he shall reign," although on the thin vowel e, I know of no better word than " angelic " to express the impression made upon the minds of the visitors present.

I said to Mr. W. H. Richardson, their teacher and conductor: " Can these be ordinary boy voices? If so, I do not quite see how you get these results." " In the first place," he replied, " we take all the care of their voices that we can. The little fellows are not allowed to shout or talk boisterously at their play or at any time, and we are constantly on the watch to keep their tones soft and sweet, and in the proper registers." " I can not think you have much trouble in that way now," I continued. " We should have trouble enough if we were to relax our watchfulness for even a few days, I assure you," he replied. I mention this conversation to show that what seemed so easy—almost spontaneous, was really the result of hard work and constant watchfulness.

After this performance came the " Swanley Boys " proper, that is, the large chorus was sent away all but about forty boys. These form the famous choir. They go about a good deal giving concerts which result in considerable pecuniary aid to the Institution. And now came beautiful part-songs in three parts, and then some blackboard "tests." Mr. Curwen gave some excellent examinations in tonic-sol-fa, and I followed with a moderately difficult three-part exercise on staffs. After they had sung it I only wished it had been three times as difficult—they made no more of it than if it had been the scale. It was another proof that tonic-sol-fa and staff notations go hand in hand in England, whatever may be thought about the matter in America.

After much kind attention from Mr. Gregory, the governor of the Institution, Mr. Richardson accompanied us to the station, where we bade him a warm farewell, and turned our faces toward the great city.

This is not the proper place to describe the great sights of London, but I will say that after much difficulty I got "into Parliament"—one day too late to hear Mr. Gladstone, but other speakers were well worth hearing. I think all strangers wonder first why the hall is so small, and second, why there is so little room for visitors. My good friend enlightened me on these points. He said: "You observed first that the speakers used the conversational tone. [This was especially observable.] That is an important factor in English oratory, and they will not have a room that requires shouting. Second, when exciting questions are up, they will not have an audience whose size would be a moral power on one side or the other, so they planned to have but few visitors at a time."

I can only hope to be excused for so much of the personal pronoun—first person, singular number—as will appear in what remains to be related of my English visit, on the ground that some of the facts, particularly those that have a bearing upon an international copyright law, will be of general interest. For the rest, I hope my readers will not be sorry to learn more particularly of the attention and kindness shown me across the water.

The day after my arrival in London a public reception was suggested, but I preferred a less formal way of meeting the musical friends, and so expressed myself to Mr. Curwen, who had the matter in charge. This resulted in an invitation, which included the conductors in and about London, who desired to meet me, to a lawn or garden party at Mr. Curwen's residence. Some were away for their vacation, but all who were accessible came, about forty in number.

I expected to be well received in England, but the reality far exceeded my expectations. All to whom I was introduced not only greeted me as an old friend, but expressed themselves in regard to my works, and their usefulness, in a way that was as unexpected as it was gratifying. Particularly was this the case on this occasion. All these gentlemen had taught and conducted my music, more or less, from the beginning of their work—indeed, as one said, some of them "had been brought up on it" before they became teachers and conductors. I did not forget, however, while these gentlemen were speaking so kindly of what I had done, and of what was still useful to them in their more elementary work, that many of their choral societies had outgrown my music and were occupied with the higher grades. An instance of this I will speak of later.

Short interviews with the friends who had so honored me was the order of the afternoon. From Mr. John Evans, superintendent of music in the public schools of London, and Mr. J. Westwood Tosh, his able assistant, I received much interesting and valuable information concerning their work; from Mr. Robert Griffiths, secretary of the tonic-sol-fa college, who remembered Dr. Mason's visit thirty-six years ago, many items of interest concerning the educational move-

ment that he had so much to do with, and from the Venables
brothers something of their work; but I leave that to an
account of a visit to their Institute, which took place a few
days later.

As the twilight drew on we adjourned to the drawing-
room (whose windows open like doors upon the lawn) and
had some music. The first number was my first song,
"Hazel Dell," sung by Mr. Sinclair Dunn, a graduate and
medalist of the Royal Academy, and a fine tenor, who sang
it in a way that made me think of Nilsson's singing of "Way
Down upon the Suwanee River." Other music, vocal and
instrumental, followed. The hearty applause which followed
a song by the writer was, he felt, simply a compliment to the
way an old man had preserved his voice. My pleasure was
greatly increased on this occasion by the presence of one of
my daughters who had been on the continent some months
with the family of a beloved nephew. She also participated
in the birthday surprise spoken of further on.

One day about this time Mr. Curwen said: "Come; I
want to show you a list of your compositions in the British
Museum." We went; and through Mr. C.'s application (he is
a member there), and by my signing a declaration that I was
more than twenty-one years of age, I became a member for
one day, with all the rights and privileges of the grandest
reading-room in the world.

We went first to a row of large books, which constitute
the musical catalogue of the place. Taking out one with
" R " on the back he turned to my name. But I should first
say that the titles of the works (songs or larger works) on
these pages are mostly written, and are pasted in with spaces
between, that, as they come, they may be put in alphabetical
order. There are, I should say, from four to six entries on
a page. First, the full name of the author, then the entire
title of the work, and by whom published. What was my

astonishment, on counting, as we turned the leaves, to find *twenty-three* pages and a part of the *twenty-fourth* occupied entirely with my compositions. I ought, perhaps, first to have explained that every publisher in the kingdom is expected to send a copy of everything he publishes to the British Museum, where it is catalogued and kept for reference.

" Now," said Mr. Curwen, " to show you how orderly and convenient their methods are here, decide what you would like to see of these works, and I will have it brought." I had been much interested to observe that " Just Before the Battle" was entered twelve times. It had been published by six different publishers, and there were six instrumental arrangements of it, so I chose an instrumental duet on that melody. ("Vacant Chair" had been entered eight times; "Tramp," seven, and others two, three, and four times.) Mr. C. then filled out a printed form, putting on it the numbers of two seats by a table, on which he left his gloves to show that the seats were taken. "Now," he said, as he handed the order to an attendant, "we will go and get lunch, and when we come back we shall find the book, with the music you want, there."

Let my reader see this picture:—a vast rotunda—the largest reading-room in the world, with hundreds of people sitting at tables, reading, studying, or copying, and scores of attendants in the alcoves or galleries getting books or returning them, and more than a million different works to be kept in their places and selected from, and he will have some idea of the perfection of the machinery necessary to keep everything running smoothly in the reading-room of the British Museum.

We had a fine lunch in the grand buffet of the building, and when we returned there was the book. It contained the duet—a good arrangement, by Brinley Richards (if I remember rightly)—and several others of my compositions, enough to fill it. Mr. Curwen fully believes in the justice of an international copyright law, and said, before I left, "You should publish a letter in some prominent paper when you return to America, stating these facts, for you are undoubtedly the greatest sufferer among the musicians there for the want of this law."

Mr. Curwen said I ought to hear one of the London choirs (choral societies). To say that, meant, with my kind host, that it should be done, if within the bounds of possibility. I think it was planned on the afternoon of the conductors' gathering, mentioned previously, with the brothers Venables. At any rate, a short time afterward I was told that, although not yet time for the gathering of the musical forces for the autumn, one of the three choirs that competed at the Crystal Palace the previous June, under the conductorship of Mr. Leonard C. Venables, would assemble to meet me at the South London Choral Institute, an institution owned and managed by the brothers.

At the time appointed we went. Although only going from one part of London to another, we had to take two trains to get there—about fifteen miles, I should judge. While the choir were gathering we were shown by Mr. George Venables the excellent appointments and many conveniences of the building, which the brothers with indomitable energy and perseverance have partially built and entirely arranged for their musical purposes. When we returned to the large hall the choir, numbering perhaps a hundred and fifty, were singing a lovely part-song. Then came one of Mendelssohn's Psalms—the one in which the solo part is taken by an alto voice. Although out of practice, as the conductor said, the performance was admirable. The young lady's voice was like Cary's, and her method charming, and the choruses were sung as only those sing who thoroughly comprehend what they are doing. The voices here, as in all the tonic-sol-fa choirs that I heard in England, were excellently taught—true and of beautiful quality.

At the conclusion of this Psalm, Mr. Venables spoke at length and most kindly of the individual whom they had gathered to meet; of the use his music had been to them; of their familiarity with it in their earlier work, etc. This gave me my key-note. Some people can talk against time —can say something interesting when they have nothing particular to say. I envy them—it is a great gift—but I can't do it. (This is no reflection upon Mr. Venables, who *had* something to say, and said it well.) I could, however, seize upon the idea that this fine choir had been in musical conditions in which my music was just what they needed and liked, and so said that I could only account for the re- ception they had given me on the ground that there are always pleasant memories connected with what we have enjoyed in earlier states, whether in social or musical life. When I alluded to their having outgrown my music, cries of "No! no! no!" came from all parts of the room. Of course that was being polite to a stranger, but I allude to it to speak of two things that interested me much in English audiences. One is that when their agreement with, or ap- proval of, the speaker is not up to the applause point, they cry "Hear! hear!" and the other is that when the disagree- ment is of a friendly kind, or not up to the hissing point in an unfriendly way, they cry "No! no!" There is some- thing more supporting and encouraging in these approving utterances than even in applause, it seems to me, probably because the sound of the human voice has in it more sym- pathy than that of hands or canes. I only regret that I did not say on that occasion what was in my heart regarding the noble enterprise which has been brought to so successful a

point by the Messrs. Venables; but I was a good deal embarrassed, and my wits did not stay by me as they should
have done.

Then came a song from my " Pilgrim Fathers " by this
lovely alto voice, and the double-theme chorus, " Blessed is
the Nation whose God is the Lord," by the whole choir.
Those interested will find the latter in " Chorus Castle," but
better in Mr. McPhail's " Crown of Song," where it has an
accompaniment written at Mr. McPhail's request.

We had so far to go that we were obliged to leave before
the exercises closed, but the kindness of these warm-hearted
friends again manifested itself by applause, which lasted until
we were out of sight and hearing.

One Sunday, toward the close of my stay, Mr. Curwen
proposed that we should go where we could hear what he
considered the best congregational singing in London—Dr.
Allon's " church," I was going to say, but I believe they call
it chapel—in Islington. We again had to take two trains to
get there. It is a large, fine church, as we should call it,
with organ behind the pulpit and galleries on three sides
converging toward the organ, without quite coming to it.
These galleries were filled with people, so that the two large
choirs which occupied the ends nearest the organ could not
in the least be distinguished from the rest of the audience.
Everybody had the same books, upstairs and down, and
when "Anthem twenty-four" was given out the burst was
so general and so full that no one could have told that a
choir of eighty voices or more was taking part. I should
not have known there was a choir at all, either by sight
or sound, if Mr. Curwen had not apprised me of the fact.
Chants, hymns (without interludes), and a still more difficult
anthem were sung heartily and all well but the chants, which
had the traditional fault before spoken of. I think the choir
do nothing alone. They do not believe in " performing " to
the people, but in singing with them.

I had a birthday while staying at Mr. Curwen's—one I shall never forget. Early on that lovely August morning the strains of Mendelssohn's "Morning Prayer" came up to my window from the lawn below. On looking out, what was my surprise to see a choir of thirty or more boys and men under the leadership of one of the conductors whom I had previously met, Mr. H. A. Donald. After this opening piece, there followed three of my little songs. When they commenced the last one I said to myself, "That's rather pretty," but did not immediately recognize it as mine. It never came to the front in America, and I had almost forgotten it. "Down where the harebells grow" is its title.

When I thanked them for the trouble they had taken, and the honor they had done me, Mr. Donald said: "Oh, we are all delighted to give you a birthday greeting—the boys, especially, have been in great excitement for a week. They sing your music a good deal, and you have come so far." I soon saw another reason for the boys' enjoyment. My kind friends, Mr. and Mrs. Curwen, of whose delicacy and attention I can not speak in adequate terms, had invited the boys, and the gentlemen who accompanied them, to breakfast. A caterer appeared as soon as the singing was over and set a table on the lawn for the boys, the gentlemen breakfasting with us in the house. The lovely grace which the boys sang before they sat down, and the three cheers they gave when they went away, will always ring in my memory when I think of that morning.

On visiting the Crystal Palace, of whose vastness words can hardly convey an adequate idea, every one is impressed with the magnitude of the arrangements for chorus performances. The great organ in the center is named "Handel," and at its sides and in front are seats in crescent form for five thousand singers, with room in the center for an orchestra of five or six hundred. I forget whether it was

Mr. Proudman, Mr. McNaught, or Mr. Venables who, when speaking of the different effects they had produced there, told me that they once gave my "Autumn Winds" in that place with forty sopranos singing the solo, and the balance of the five thousand humming the accompaniment—the vast audience being greatly excited over the result.

The only remaining thing to note was a concert, with "readings," on the steamship *City of Rome* coming home. It was for the benefit of some seamen's charitable association, and given by such musical people and elocutionists as happened to be on board. I tried to keep out of the way and let the younger people do the performing, but they found me out, and I had to take part. When my turn came I sang "The Sea," as appropriate to the occasion. The applause which followed brought the chairman to his feet, who, in a very kind and complimentary speech, gave a list of my principal songs, beginning "way back." When he came to naming and speaking of the war songs, one by one, there was a manifest commotion in the thronged cabin and gangways, and when he wound up with "Battle-Cry" and "Tramp," the whole company gave three ringing cheers. It turned out that there were quite a number of army people among the crowd of returning Americans. After the great kindness of my English friends, it was pleasant to find, after all, that "a prophet" may have some "honor in his own country."

CHAPTER XVIII.

HOME AGAIN—THE "PILLAR OF FIRE" AND OTHER CANTATAS
—THE IDEA OF "CANTATAS FOR THE PEOPLE"—MR. AND
MRS. J. S. CURWEN'S VISIT TO AMERICA — "WAR-SONG"
CONCERTS—THE LOYAL LEGION—THE USUAL HISTORY OF
MUSICAL SOCIETIES—HOW "THE HAYMAKERS" HELPED
OUT—FAMILY MATTERS, "ROOTS AND BRANCHES"—THE
HYDE PARK YACHT CLUB AND THE SUMMER CONGREGA-
TION ON THE LAKE.

MY first work on my return was to carry out a plan for
a cantata suggested by Mr. Hall, of the London Sunday-School Union—the return of Israel from the captivity
in Egypt. Mr. Butterworth helped in the words, and "The
Pillar of Fire" was the result, though they call it "Cloud
and Sunshine" in England.

I made the acquaintance of Mr. John Stuart Bogg, a poet
and author, while attending a New Church conference in
Lancashire, and on my return he sent me a libretto for a
Sunday-school and choir cantata, called "The Building of
the Temple"; then followed librettos by other well-known
English librettists—"Bethlehem," by Frederic E.Weatherly;
"Florens, the Pilgrim," by David Gow; and "Jacob and
Esau," by A. J. Foxwell. These I have set to music, and
they are published in London in connection with the Cin-
cinnati house.

For Christmas, 1886, my daughter, Clara Louise Burnham, and I wrote "The Waifs' Christmas," and for Christmas, 1887, "Judge Santa Claus." In 1888 we wrote "Snow
White and the Seven Dwarfs," a cantata in which the cho-

ruses are for children and the solo parts for adult voices; and for Christmas, 1889, " Santa Claus & Co." These cantatas are also published in England, though in some cases under different names.

My other works since my return are " The Repertoire," for High-Schools; " The Empire of Song," and " The Arena of Song," (the latter with Mr. C. C. Case,) for musical conventions; " The Glorious Cause," for temperance work, and a little cantata for Sunday-schools called " The Wonderful Story," the libretto by Mrs. Mary B. Brooks, of Arkansas.

It is interesting to note the popularity of the idea of " cantatas for the people." We know at once what is meant when we say " songs for the people." In that sense I use the term " cantatas for the people." They began with " The Flower Queen," " Daniel," and " The Haymakers," as representatives of the three kinds—juvenile, scriptural and secular. They have multiplied greatly of late years, especially in England. Mr. Curwen spoke to me while I was at his house about sending me librettos when he should find those that he thought would suit me. This he has done, as above mentioned, and I am now at work upon others. This brings the record of my principal compositions up to 1890.

In the autumn of 1887 we had a visit from Mr. and Mrs. J. S. Curwen, and no one who met them wondered at their popularity and success as leaders of a great musical movement in England. I mention Mrs. Curwen's name in this connection, because to his general culture and remarkable gifts as a leader she adds such attainments, both musical and literary, as must count for much in the success of their enterprises. It was a great pleasure to return some of their kindness, and to note their friendly and unprejudiced interest in our American ways. That visit is a theme of which my family never tire.

I have said that when the war closed all interest in the

war songs ceased. For years they were out of sight, but now that time has changed the terrible realism of the march and the battle-field into tender and hallowed memories, the songs that were then sung have come back with redoubled interest. Their melodies are heard on all patriotic occasions and the most deeply stirred and enthusiastic audiences of the present time are those of the " war-song concerts." I have especially in mind a concert of this kind that was given not long ago by the Apollo Club of Chicago, under the direction of Wm. L. Tomlins. I directed the performance of "Yes, we'll rally round the flag, boys," (The Battle-Cry of Freedom) on that occasion, and as I came forward, said: " Here is the man [J. G. Lumbard] who twenty-five years ago sang that song on the court-house steps before the ink of the manuscript was dry. He will sing it now. Will all join in the chorus?" Jule's magnificent voice rang out just as it had done a quarter of a century before. The immense audience rose and, impelled by their intense emotion, joined with the band and the grand chorus of the Apollo Club, producing an effect never to be forgotten.

Soon after that demonstration I was elected a member of the Loyal Legion, but I will let Mr. Murray's article, in *The Musical Visitor* which followed, tell the story. Being in the war himself, he was in a condition to write it from a soldier's standpoint.

THE LOYAL LEGION AND DR. ROOT.

The readers of the *Visitor* will be interested in the following notes concerning Dr. Root's initiation into the " Loyal Legion," a society of noble men who have in this case honored themselves as well as the recipient of their very exclusive favors.

The " Loyal Legion " is the highest of the military and patriotic organizations of the country. The people eligible to membership in it are, in the first class—Commissioned officers who were in the war, and whose record then and since is satisfactory ; second class—Their oldest sons on arriving at the age of twenty-one; third class—Civilians who rendered "important service" during the war. This last membership is limited. There are but six in the Illinois Commandery, which has over two hundred members. (General Sheridan was the commander-in-chief of the Order at the time of his death.)

A little over a year ago the former president of the Illinois Sanitary Commission died, and a month ago Dr. George F. Root was elected to fill the vacancy caused by his removal.

If there is any civilian who performed "important service" for the Union during the war, Dr. Root is that man. The editor of the *Visitor* was in the field during all the hardest fighting of the war, and had abundant opportunity to prove the above assertion true. The late testimonials in *The Century* magazine from men and officers concerning the wonderful effect of Dr. Root's "War Songs" also fully substantiate our claim. But then this fact is heartily acknowledged everywhere, and nowhere more completely than in the "Loyal Legion," as may be seen from the fact that a single objection to a candidate of this class, by a line drawn through the name on the ballot, settles the question and excludes the candidate. In this case the election was, as the senator from Kansas in his late celebrated speech said of another election, "more than unanimous."

A member has said that seldom if ever has a name been received by the Order with so much enthusiasm as greeted this one. Those familiar with the customs of the Order can very well see why this would be so. After the business and "refreshments" of the evening are through, the members gather together to sing the old war songs. Staid generals, colonels, majors, captains, chaplains, and all, become boys again, and, with the intense sphere of the old days about them, pour forth such a volume of patriotic earnestness as can only be appreciated by those who connect those melodies with camp, the march, and the battle-field. It is easy to see why the man who had to do with the making of those songs was so kindly received and heartily welcomed.

Of course the Doctor was asked to sing. He responded with "Yes, we'll rally round the flag," undoubtedly the strongest of his war lyrics. The editor of the *Visitor* heard this song once, when in the outer line of intrenchments before Petersburg, within talking distance of the Confederate line of battle. He never expects to hear it sung again as it was sung at that time, but the nearest approach to it would be to hear it sung by the "boys" who were there, who now compose these patriotic societies. Here are the men who shouted

that line when the next minute they might have to give their lives
for the Union they were fighting to maintain.   It is not to be wondered at that their interest in the old songs is so strong.   They were
the companions of their camp-fires, their cheer on many long and
weary marches, and their inspiration sometimes on the very field of
battle.

The attachments and associations of the war are all very strong.
While the animosities have nearly all disappeared between Union
and Confederates, we can see very clearly how each still retains love
and affection for its leaders and for each other and for the old songs,
and for those who wrote them. We congratulate the " Loyal Legion "
on making so worthy an addition to its membership.   The *Visitor*
is inclined to indulge in a little personal pride in the matter, as Dr.
Root is so prominent a member of its family.

Speaking of the Apollo Club brings to mind the musical
organization that I found when I came to Chicago in 1859.
It was called the Musical Union, and was conducted by Mr.
Cady ; but soon business required all of Mr. Cady's time, and
the conduct of the society passed into other hands.   The
history of musical societies is pretty uniform.   A few insist
in the outset upon practicing music beyond the ability of the
chorus to perform, and of the audience to enjoy, and both
drop off.   Then come debt and appeals to the consciences
of the chorus, and the purses of the patrons, to sustain a
worthy (?) enterprise.   Then follows a lingering death—and
all because a few leading members will not give up the difficult music they like best, for the simple music that can be
well sung and so enjoyed.   The Musical Union was no exception to this rule, only it did not reach the extremity mentioned above.   It traveled the usual path until it had become
nearly a thousand dollars in debt, and then it stopped to
think.   Some one suggested that instead of appealing to the
people for help, that it might be a good plan to try to please
them, and so get them to pay because they desired to, and
not because they ought to.   In this exigency they asked me
to give " The Haymakers," which I was very happy to do

Two performances cleared off the debt, and left a small balance in the treasury. A musical organization of some kind has existed ever since—sometimes two or three of them, but with no marked success until Mr. Tomlins came in 1875 and started with the Apollo Club. This was at first a male-voice chorus; after a while women's voices were added. With some of the usual mistakes, and with some fluctuations, it has held on; and under Mr. Tomlins' fine leadership has become one of the best choruses in this or any other country.

When I started out in 1838, more than fifty years ago, I was the oldest, and my sister Fanny, then a baby, the youngest, of a family of eight—three boys and five girls. There are eight still, and we still say "the boys" and "the girls"; but considering the grandfathers and grandmothers among us, others might not regard those terms as quite appropriate. My father died in 1866, and then came a contest for the dear mother. All wanted her, and she, wishing to gratify all, was sometimes with one or another of her sons, and sometimes with one of her daughters. I do not know how many journeys she made from Boston or New York to Chicago, but a good many. Finally, as she approached the age of four score, she decided upon the house of her oldest daughter in Orange, N. J., as her home, and here she lived most happily, passing away in 1881, in the eighty-fifth year of her age. If any of her children could have settled down in North Reading she would have stayed at Willow Farm, but as that could not be, she decided that the old place had better be sold, which was done soon after she left it. She was so inexpressibly dear to her children that to "rise and call her blessed" is ever in our minds, when we think of her loving and unselfish life.

My branch of the family consists of wife, two married sons, three married daughters and one unmarried, and eleven grandchildren. All live near, excepting Charles, my second son, and family, who are in the neighborhood of New York, into which city the young man goes daily to superintend certain publications of which he is proprietor.

My oldest son, Frederic W., and family live, as do all the rest of us, in Hyde Park, near Chicago. If this young man is better equipped musically and otherwise than his father was at his age, there is more need now than there was then, of higher attainment. In these days of greater demand, one only reaches the position that he occupies as a musician, teacher and writer, by beginning in advance of the previous generation and then super-adding to his inheritance, years of close study and hard work. It would be pleasant to give some account of his very successful and remunerative work, but that would hardly be proper here. I will, however, say that he teaches and writes ten months in the year, and then in the summer, when he is not at Normal, is the bold and hardy navigator of a cat-boat on the broad waters of Lake Michigan, where he stores up air and sunshine for his winter campaign.

My children were all inclined more or less to music as a profession as they were growing up, and all are considerably above mediocrity as players or singers ; but F. W. is the only one who has persisted in the original inclination. My oldest daughter, Mrs. Clara Louise Burnham, is not unknown to fame as a writer of good books of fiction, and I venture to speak further of this member of my family, because her career illustrates a point in my own case to which I have two or three times alluded.

After her marriage, Mrs. Burnham, having a good deal of leisure and no family cares, felt a desire for some especial occupation. One day her brother F. W. said : " Write a book, Clara ; anybody who can write so good a letter as you can, can write a good story." She certainly never felt that she had a " call " in that direction, but she tried it, and has had no heavy hours upon her hands since that time.

My younger daughters are much interested in art, in which they are fairly successful, not neglecting, however, their musical studies.

Of the clan in general, including brothers and sisters, nephews and nieces, and the families with which they are connected, living near, it is only necessary to sound the call and more than thirty respond. All are musical—the children of my brother E. T. conspicuously so. They occupy some of the best choir positions in the city, and one of the young ladies is one of Chicago's best amateur pianists. One of our modes of enjoyment is worth mentioning: Nearly all are members of the Hyde Park Yacht Club, whose fine boat-house is close by. On calm summer evenings a small fleet drifts out a half mile or so from shore, and a song commences—

> "Sweet and low, sweet and low,
> Wind of the western sea,"

or some other in which all can join. Then the congregation begins to assemble. Boats shoot out from all along the coast until we are surrounded by a sympathetic and appreciative audience. The whole fleet is then held together by lines or hands, and we drift, sometimes up toward the city, sometimes down toward the great park, and sometimes farther out into the "saltless sea," just as the current or the light breeze may take us, but " making music as we go," and enjoying to the full the luxury of the lovely scene. Our boats and the companionship of the club are a great resource in the summer.

CHAPTER XIX.

THE JOHN CHURCH CO.—THE PRINCIPALS OF THE HOUSE—
THEIR HOMES—ANCESTRAL DESCENT—THE MEMORABLE
CELEBRATION AT THE HYDE PARK HIGH-SCHOOL—MR.
JOHN CHURCH'S DEATH—PREPARATIONS FOR THE WORLD'S
COLUMBIAN EXPOSITION—MY PIANO TRADE—MY SEVEN-
TIETH BIRTHDAY—*VALE!*

THERE are some people who seem to have been forced
by circumstances into the wrong niche in this world,
and whose work, in consequence, is a dread in the anticipa-
tion and a drudgery in the performance. I am humbly
thankful that that has not been my lot. My work has always
been my greatest pleasure, and still is. If I was for a time
crowded into a niche that belonged to somebody else, all
that passed away when we arranged with the John Church
Co., as already described. From that time, as I have said,
my business cares vanished, and I have been occupied in
the congenial work of making such books, cantatas, songs
or numbers for their Annuals (Christmas and Easter Selections, etc.) or *The Musical Visitor*, as are thought needful,
while they attend to all the business matters connected with
these works—copyrights, arrangements with English publishers, permissions, etc.

Mr. Church, the founder of this house, and Mr. Trevor,
his long-time partner, may well be proud of its success, for
that success, as I have abundant reason to know, is founded
upon the most honorable business principles and the most
upright business transactions. I may not speak in detail of
their arrangement with me, nor of the many generous acts

which have characterized our years of relationship, but I should be recreant to my sense of right if I did not take this opportunity to record my appreciation of their unvarying kindness and consideration, and of my great satisfaction in doing all in my power for their interests.

When the May Festival, or other errand, calls me to Cincinnati, it is a great pleasure to enjoy the hospitality of Mr. Trevor's beautiful home on Mt. Auburn, or in the summer to be a guest at Mr. Church's old colonial residence in Rhode Island. Ancestral descent is not a strong point with the majority of American people, nor are many situated in localities of historic interest; but in Mr. Church's case both these conditions obtain in a remarkable degree. Not far away from his residence is Mt. Hope, where King Philip, of the Narragansetts, lived and fought, and back from Mr. John Church, in an unbroken line, is Capt. Benjamin Church, who defeated the great chief and brought the famous war called " King Philip's War " to a close.

The present house stands on ground deeded to the family in 1674, and in the establishment rare skill and taste have been shown in combining modern elegance and convenience with the old colonial architecture and surroundings. In plain sight from Mr. Church's residence is also the spot where John Alden and his wife Priscilla Mullins lived. This Priscilla, it will be remembered, was the maiden made famous in Longfellow's poem, " The Courtship of Miles Standish." Both she and John came over in the *May Flower*. In the village church-yard are the grave and monument of their daughter Elizabeth, who was the first white female child born in the colony. She married William Peabody, and died at the age of 94 in 1717.

And now I am approaching the end of my story, but I can not close without recording a recent event which was as unexpected as it will ever be memorable. We have in Hyde

Park one of the finest high-schools in the state, not only as to building, but equally as to faculty and pupils. They use there one of my books for their musical studies, and one day one of the teachers asked me if I would come some afternoon and listen to a program to consist entirely of my works. I said I should be glad to do so, and the 8th of March, 1889, was fixed upon for the event. It would be hard to find a more astonished individual than the writer, on arriving at the scene of action. It was a series of surprises from beginning to end. First the crowd, then the decorations, then the performances, then the letters and speeches of distinguished people, winding up with the congratulations of neighbors and friends; but I will let the published reports describe the occasion. If it is thought that I am printing too much praise of myself, I have only to say that I can not otherwise record the great kindness of the friends who so honored me. Beside, the event took on something of a public character, from the fact that the Associated Press despatches made it known all over the land, as the letters from many states, which followed, abundantly testified. Chicago papers the next day said:

At the Hyde Park High-School Dr. George F. Root was the recipient, yesterday afternoon, of all the honor the two hundred students and their teachers and two hundred more friends and admirers could well bestow. The spacious hall of the building was profusely decorated with flags and banners, and on its walls were tablets in a variety of colors, bearing the names of his best-known compositions, each with an appropriate design. On the platform were stacked old army muskets in threes, and in the cradles formed by the bayonets rested birds' nests, emblematical of a united and peaceful country. At the left of the platform was a war relic in the shape of an army tent, in front of which burned a miniature camp-fire; bunches of swords here and there, and an excellent portrait of Dr. Root, draped in national colors and hung over the platform, completed the ornamentations. The musical exercises consisted of the performance of vocal and instrumental numbers selected from Dr.

Root's compositions, and of the ode printed below, which last was composed by one of the teachers of the school. These exercises were interspersed by papers composed and read by members of the school on various subjects connected with the Doctor's life and works, and by the following letters from distinguished individuals, which were in response to invitations to the celebration, sent by one of the teachers of the school. That from James Russell Lowell is as follows:

No. 68 BEACON ST., BOSTON, MASS.

It is impossible for me to be present at your interesting celebration, but I remember too well the martial cadences of Dr. Root's songs, and how vividly our hearts beat in tune to them, not to add gladly my felicitations to yours. I prize gratitude highly, and you could not have chosen a fitter creditor to whom it should be paid, or a better form in which to pay it. Pray add mine to your own.

Yours faithfully,
J. R. LOWELL.

The present Governor of Illinois writes:

I count it a privilege to be permitted to join the scholars of the Hyde Park High-School in a tribute to Dr. George F. Root. Only those who were at the front, camping, marching, battling for the flag, can fully realize how often we were cheered, revived and inspired by the songs of him who sent forth the "Battle-Cry of Freedom." The true and correct history of the war for the maintenance of the Union will place George F. Root's name alongside of our great generals. While others led the boys in blue to final victory, it was his songs that nerved the men at the front and solaced the wives, mothers, sisters, and sweethearts at home, while more than a million voices joined in the chorus, "The Union forever."

Will you please convey to your distinguished guest my kindest regards and best wishes.   Sincerely yours,
J. W. FIFER.

Col. Fred. Grant writes:

The author of "Rally round the flag, boys," and "Tramp, tramp, tramp, the boys are marching," should have as hearty a welcome as it is possible to extend to any living man. His songs were a great comfort to the soldiers during the war, and helped to lighten the fatigues of many a weary march. Tell Dr. Root that I am grateful for the service he rendered.

F. D. GRANT.

Rev. S. F. Smith, D. D., author of "My country, 'tis of thee," says:

It gives me unalloyed pleasure to speak a word or two in honor of the man whose genius has given to his countrymen, and to the world, the inspiring lays, "Rally round the flag, boys," "Tramp,

Tramp, Tramp," and "Shining Shore." There is no greater honor or privilege than to have attuned the harp of the nation to words and tunes of patriotic zeal, and the harps of the world to a music which beats time to the march of a redeemed race to a holy and happy heaven.

May your honored guest long listen to the music of that march, and find his path ever growing more luminous with the light from that Shining Shore.

With assurances of sincere respect and honor to him, and the best wishes for your pupils, that some of them may rise up in his spirit to carry forward his work, I am,

Very sincerely yours,

S. F. SMITH.

Edward Everett Hale, whose response came too late to be read on that occasion, wrote from Washington as follows:

Dear Sir: Your note has followed me here. I hope this may be in time for me to join with the rest of the world in thanking Dr. Root for the strength, courage and life he has given to us all.

Very truly yours,

EDWARD E. HALE.

The response of J. G. Lumbard, Esq., now of Omaha, whose magnificent voice was the first to give utterance to the "Battle-Cry of Freedom," was also too late to be read on the day of the celebration, but was subsequently published in one of our local papers.

Dear Sir: I am most certainly and most sincerely in sympathy with the movement inaugurated at Hyde Park, looking to an appropriate recognition of the good service and unusual desert of our mutual friend and *confrère,* Dr. Geo. F. Root, and I very much regret that the delayed arrival of your invitation prevents its acceptance or any timely response. It came to hand on the day of the event.

No words of mine can add anything to the glory and beauty of a well-spent life, nor give increased lustre to the shining character of one whose career has been that of a universal benefactor.

It is not alone the community in which he has lived and exercised the rights and discharged the responsibilities of citizenship, that owes a debt of honor and gratitude to Dr. Root: the whole people have been educated to a nobler patriotism and higher citizenship by the illustrated virtues of his life, and the beneficent influence of his character and teachings.

We honor the great soldier by whose genius and prowess the way has been carved to victory and peace; but greater than the soldier is he who prevents appeal to arms, and preserves our green fields for lawns instead of devoting them to grave-yards for the brave. All this, without noise and without pretense, has been done by the gentleman to whom it is honorable to pay honor and homage.

If opportunity offers, please express from me the kindest remembrance to Dr. Root, and regret at my inability to be present in accordance with the terms of your invitation.

Yours very truly,

J. G. LUMBARD.

Several other communications, including a few words from Generals Sherman and Alger, were also received. Some war reminiscences from Dr. H. H. Belfield, formerly Adjutant of the Iowa Cavalry Volunteers, now principal of the Chicago Manual Training School, were listened to with great interest and with general surprise, for but few of those present knew that he had been a soldier and a prisoner during the eventful time of which he speaks. He said:

It affords me great pleasure to unite in this testimonial to our neighbor, Dr. Root, whose character as well as whose life-work commands our admiration.

The overthrow of the enemies of the Republic in the late war was a stupendous undertaking, demanding the supreme effort of the loyal North, not only of the men who took the field, but of the men and women who remained at home. Not men alone were needed, but arms, ammunition, clothing and food; not material support only, but sympathy as well. The Union soldier was cheered by many kind and loving messages from the yearning, often aching, hearts of wives and children, of parents and friends. How precious was the consciousness of this remembrance can be known only by those who tore themselves from the fond embrace of loved ones to endure the hardship of the march, and face the grim terrors of the bloody field.

Among the friends who, in those awful years, served his country effectually, more effectually by his pen than any man could have done by his sword, was Dr. George F. Root. You have heard to-day how his songs encouraged our troops even in that frightful campaign near Richmond. Permit me to tell briefly how they cheered the prisoners of war.

It was the 31st day of July, 1864, in Newnan, Georgia. The starry banner with which you, my young friends, have so beautifully decorated this room, had gone down in blood and death ; the hated rebel rag was flying in triumph over the heads of a small company of Union soldiers, who, having obeyed the orders that they well knew would sacrifice them, had saved hundreds of their comrades, and were now prisoners of war. Their appearance showed the effects of hard campaigning—bronzed faces, torn and ragged garments, with here and there a rough bandage stained with blood. But their spirits were undaunted, and as the populace gathered around them, curious to see the hated Yankees, and, perhaps, to exult over their ill fortune, the little band sang the patriotic songs which had been wafted from " God's Country."

When we sang, with all the emphasis of which we were capable,

> " Rally round the flag, boys ;
> Down with the *traitor !* "

I fully expected marked symptoms of disapproval ; but the increasing crowd seemed to enjoy the novel spectacle, and, when we ceased singing, shouted for more songs. Then we said, " We are tired ; we are hungry ; we have had no food for many hours. Give us something to eat, and we will sing for you." Food was soon brought, and I now take this opportunity, long delayed, to thank *you*, Doctor Root, for what, while it could not be called " a square meal," is well and gratefully remembered after these many years.

The latter part of the summer of 1864 I spent, together with several hundred Union officers, at the sea-side, at the expense of the Southern Confederacy. The place selected for our temporary retirement from active life was Charleston, S. C. Three hundred of us were in the work-house prison, in what particular part of the city located I never knew, since the wishes of our hosts, expressed in high walls and southern muskets, prevented our exploring the town. But we knew that the sea was near, for the huge, fifteen-inch shells of the " Swamp Angel," screaming over our heads, scattered brick and mortar over the grass-grown streets of the hot-bed of the Rebellion.

Late one afternoon in September our attention was directed to the entrance of men into the adjoining prison-yard. We rushed to

the windows on that side of the prison-house, and anxiously in-
spected the new comers. With faces blacked by sun and stained
with dirt, their clothing scant and torn, they wearily dragged themselves into the prison-pen. Before they came within speaking distance the faded army blue of their uniforms suggested the truth.
"Who are you?" we asked. "Andersonville prisoners." May I never
behold another such sight. Their piercing eyes, their emaciated
features, their shrunken limbs, now concealed, now revealed by their
ragged uniforms, their bloody bandages, told the awful story of slow
starvation. We shared with them our scanty rations, and after a
frugal meal on each side of the wall, which neither party could
cross, we did all we could for them; we sang Doctor Root's songs,
and cheered their hearts with our sympathy. Never had poor performers so attentive an audience. Long into the night we sang, and
in the early morning we dismissed them, Doctor Root, with your
ringing chorus, in which their feeble voices were heard—

> " Tramp, tramp, tramp, the boys are marching,
> Cheer up, comrades, they *will* come ;
> And beneath the starry flag we shall breathe the air again
> Of the free-land in our own beloved home."

The following Ode was most effectively rendered by a
semi-chorus of the students, all the school coming in, after
the first verse, with the chorus of "There's music in the
air," after the second, with the chorus of the "Battle-Cry,"
and after the third, with the chorus of the "Shining Shore."

THE SINGER OF HOME.

Happy is he
Whose ears have heard the sound
Of music from glad voices singing
Songs himself has made.
From sea to sea,
Wherever home is found,
His loved refrains are ever ringing
Clear in grove and glade.

Chorus: There's music in the air.

THE MAKER OF WAR SONGS.

Proud is the man
Whose words can nerve the arm
Of freemen to their noblest trying,
And urge them on ;
From rear to van
His war songs' loud alarm
Inspired the living, cheered the dying,
Till war was gone.
Chorus: The Union forever!

THE WRITER OF HYMNS.

How nobly best
Is he who puts to song
The comfort of the weary ; driving
Sorrow's tears away.
Sweet peace and rest
Unto his lays belong
Which sing of end to toil and striving
Some glorious day.
Chorus: For oh, we stand on Jordan's strand.

Then came a toast to which I was obliged to respond. I could not make much of a speech. The difference between "Come down some afternoon and hear us sing," and this magnificent demonstration, was too much for me. However, I could say that such an occasion was a great reward, and a great encouragement for me in my work, and that I should never forget the young people and their teachers who had so honored me.

To Mr. Ray, the principal of the school, and to Mr. McAndrew, whose invitations called forth the foregoing responses, and who composed the Ode, and to Mr. Stevens, whose artistic hand was seen in the beautiful decorations of the hall, I could express more fully my surprise at the amount of work that teachers and pupils had done, and the deep and thankful pride I felt at being so honored by my neighbors.

It is now 1891. Most of this story, as I have said, was written in 1889. Of the persons mentioned, who have died since that time, the most important in its connection with these records was the death of Mr. John Church, which took place April 19, 1890.

In connection with what is said of Mr. Church in its proper place, I would like to add here the few words I wrote for *The Musical Visitor* at the time of the sudden bereavement. We heard of his illness one day, and of his death the next.

One of Nature's noblemen has gone; and gone with such suddenness that we gaze after his vanishing form as in a dream. It does not seem possible that we shall not see again that stalwart form, nor feel again the friendly grasp of that strong hand. We could not readily connect death with him, he was so full of vigor as he carried on, in his masterful way, the important enterprises in which he was engaged.

From the dark days that followed the great fire, when the strong house of which Mr. Church was chief, took hold of and sustained us in the crippled state in which the great disaster left us, to the time of his death he was a true friend—kind without pretension, and generous without ostentation; a wise counselor and a safe guide. Among my most valued memories will be those of this noble man.

The wisdom of the house in forming itself into a stock company three or four years ago, was clearly seen at the time of this sad event. Not a ripple disturbed the onward flow of its business; all goes as before, so far as I can see.

Chicago is a very interesting place just now. We are getting ready for the World's Fair, or better, as it is beginning to be called, "The World's Columbian Exposition." The inner and the outer world here—the world of mind and the world of matter, are intensely alive, devising plans of use and enjoyment, which are beginning to ultimate themselves in visible forms.

Among the new plans is "The Auxiliary Commission of the World's Columbian Exposition," which has for its motto "Not Things, but Men." I will let its prospectus state its object:

As is now well known, the four hundredth anniversary of the discovery of America by Christopher Columbus will be celebrated at Chicago in 1893, under the sanction of the Government of the United States, on a scale commensurate with the importance and dignity of the occasion.

The measures already taken give satisfactory assurances that the exposition then to be made of the material progress of the world will be such as to deserve unqualified approval.

But to make the exposition complete and the celebration adequate, the wonderful achievements of the new age in science, literature, education, government, jurisprudence, morals, charity, religion, and other departments of human activity, should also be conspicuously displayed, as the most effective means of increasing the fraternity, prosperity, and peace of mankind.

It has therefore been proposed that a series of *World's Congresses* for that purpose be held in connection with the World's Columbian Exposition of 1893, and THE WORLD'S CONGRESS AUXILIARY has been duly authorized and organized, to promote the holding and success of such congresses.

It is impossible to estimate the advantages that would result from the mere establishment of personal acquaintance and friendly relations among the leaders of the intellectual and moral world, who now, for the most part, know each other only through the interchange of publications, and, perhaps, the formalities of correspondence.

And what is transcendently more important, such congresses, convened under circumstances so auspicious, would doubtless surpass all previous efforts to bring about a real fraternity of nations, and unite the enlightened people of the whole earth in a general co-operation for the attainment of the great ends for which human society is organized.

This organization is intended to promote the success of the exposition of the material products of civilization, science and art, but will confine its own operations to the exposition, in appropriate conventions, of the principles of human progress.

CHARLES C. BONNEY,   LYMAN J. GAGE,
          President.   *Treasurer.*
THOMAS B. BRYAN,   BENJAMIN BUTTERWORTH,
          Vice-President.   *Secretary.*

These congresses will be held at such times, during the Exposition, as will be most convenient to each.

Considerable importance has been attached to the assembling of a Musical Congress on this occasion, which shall include prominent musicians and musical educators of this and other countries. I am one of the five members of the commission chosen for the furtherance of this object.

One of the greatest causes of excitement at present in Chicago, in view of the coming World's Exposition, is the real estate "boom" now upon us. The land romances, as they might almost be called, of earlier times, are being re-enacted every day. Every old resident has one or more to tell.

In the "earlier times" a man took a piece of ground out on the prairie for a small debt, or he let a friend have a piano or other article of merchandise for a lot or two. Such property was regarded as of little consequence. Almost every business man had some. While for one reason or another (the great fire a prominent one) I have failed to hold on to the large amounts of money which have been realized from my music, some of these small patches of Chicago ground that had been in my possession many years, when the decision in regard to the World's Fair was made known, came to the front, and were disposed of in a way to entitle the transaction to a place in the romances referred to.

I will not enlarge upon my seventieth birthday celebration, farther than to say it was intended to be simply and wholly a family affair, but my friends of the Chicago papers got wind of it, and the reporters and the Associated Press despatches did the rest. Gifts and congratulations from home and abroad poured in most generously, and the autograph stream, which, if small is, in general, remarkably steady, grew into a freshet, which did not subside for three or four weeks.

Of all the communications received on that occasion a poem by Mr. Murray, which was printed about that time in *The Musical Visitor,* moved me most. I do not deserve it, and it pushes the appearance of self-praise, of which I have spoken, to the very verge of propriety for me to print it, but it is so fine in itself, and is so pleasant an event in my story, that I decide it must go in with the other kind and generous things which have done so much toward making my life a happy and thankful one.

TO DR. GEO. F. ROOT.

ON HIS SEVENTIETH BIRTHDAY.

Dear Master and friend, I salute you!
The sapling bends low to the oak-tree,
And I am but one in a forest
Of those who would fain do you homage.
Your years have been many and blessed,
Though mingled with sunshine and shadow,
The life spent in service for others
Dwells not in the regions of darkness.

How grand are the gifts of the singer,
Whose voice tuned to thoughts that are noble
Sends out to the world in its sorrow
The music that lightens its labor.
How brightens the eye of the lover
When song in sweet notes tells his story.
How firm is the tread of the soldier
When song nerves his soul for the battle.
So far o'er the wastes of the waters
The wanderer sings of his homeland,

And cheered by the music of childhood,
Forgets all the pain and the toiling.

Thus up from the labor of earthland
He gazes whose home is in Heaven,
And sings as he works, as he wanders,
Of those who await his home-coming.

All these, dearest master, salute you,
And hosts of the sweet little children,
Whose studies your music made easy,
As climbing the hill of Parnassus
They leaned on the staff you provided.

How noble, how grand was the mission
The Master of Music assigned you,
To tune all the tongues of the people
To strains that were helpful and holy.
To guide like a voice in the darkness
The feet of the lonely and straying,
To cheer the forlorn and the weary,
To sing away tears from the weeping.

And what shall the end be, and guerdon,
For years full of blessing and beauty?
"Well done, faithful servant, come higher;
Come up to the music eternal!"

Pass on to the Land of the Singers,
O sweetest of all the Musicians.
Afar from the Valley of Shadows,
Up, up to the Brightness and Glory.
Away o'er the Mountains of Beauty,
Whose tops all aglow with the shining
And sheen of the Gates of the City,
Make light all the way of the journey.
Sing on to the close of the journey,
Sing ever when it shall be ended,
For they who have lessened earth's sorrows
Have songs in their hearts through the ages.

Dear Master and friend, I salute you!

JAMES R. MURRAY.

To conclude, I can not imagine a pleasanter life for myself than the one I now live. When not at normals or conventions, I work at home, because in the city I should be liable to frequent interruptions. My working-room is at the top of the house, to be as far from the parlor and the piano as possible, but the view from this elevation is an abundant compensation for the trouble of reaching it. I have only to raise my eyes to look east over the ever-changing waters of the lake, or north over one of its bays to the city center, seven miles away. Mr. E. V. Church, of whom I have spoken, is still manager of the Chicago house, and I am at my pleasant quarters in his establishment at a certain hour every day, in case any one wishes to see me, and at other times if I am wanted, or need a rest from my work. More than fifty trains pass each way every day, and the lovely ride by the lake can not be equaled, I think, in the world.

My wife and I would be glad to be permitted to see our golden wedding-day, which will be in 1895, and still more, to look over into the twentieth century, which will be five years later; but if that can not be, we will be thankful for the pleasant life we have lived here, and hope for a pleasanter and still more useful life hereafter.

APPENDIX.

FOLLOWING are lists of my books and of nearly all my sheet-music compositions. Then come the two part-songs spoken of in my story as having been sung by my Quartet. Then two of my compositions of a medium grade of difficulty (there is not room for a specimen of the more difficult ones, "The Storm Chorus" in "The Haymakers" for example), then the best known of my "People's Songs."

BOOKS.

The Young Ladies' Choir . 1847
Root & Sweetzer's Collection,1849
Academy Vocalist 1852
The Flower Queen 1852
The Shawm (with W. B. Brad-
    bury) 1853
Daniel 1853
The Pilgrim Fathers . . . 1854
The Young Men's Singing
    Book 1855
The Musical Album 1855
The Sabbath Bell 1856
The Haymakers 1857
The Festival Glee Book . . 1859
Belshazzar's Feast 1860
The Diapason 1860
The Silver Chime 1862

The Christian Graces . . . 1862
The Silver Lute 1862
School for Cabinet Organ . 1863
The Bugle Call 1863
The Musical Curriculum . . 1864
The New Coronet 1865
The Cabinet Organ Compan-
    ion 1865
The Guide to the Pianoforte 1865
Our Song Birds (4 small pam-
    phlets) 1866
The Forest Choir 1867
The Musical Fountain . . . 1867
Chapel Gems 1868
The Triumph 1868
The Prize 1870
The Glory 1872

The Hour of Praise 1872

The Normal Musical Hand-
book 1872

The New Musical Curricu-
lum 1872

The Männerchor 1873

The Model Organ Method . 1873

The Trumpet of Reform . 1874

The Song Era 1874

The National School Singer 1875

The Choir and Congrega-
tion 1875

The New Song Era 1877

The Song Tournament . . 1878

First Years in Song-Land . 1879

The Palace of Song 1879

The New Choir and Congre-
gation 1879

The Young Organist at
Home 1880

The Chorus Castle 1880

Under the Palms 1880

The New Flower Queen . . 1880

The Teachers' Club 1881

David, the Shepherd Boy . 1882

The Realm of Song 1882

Pure Delight (with C. C.
Case) 1883

Catching Kriss Kringle . . 1883

The Choicest Gift 1883

Our Song World (with C. C.
Case) 1884

Santa Claus' Mistake . . . 1885

Wondrous Love (with C. C.
Case) 1885

The Name Ineffable 1886

Flower Praise 1886

The Waifs' Christmas . . . 1886

Faith Triumphant 1886

The Empire of Song . . . 1887

The Repertoire 1887

Judge Santa Claus . . . 1887

The Pillar of Fire 1887

The Glorious Cause 1888

Snow White and the Seven
Dwarfs 1888

Building the Temple . . 1889

Santa Claus & Co. 1889

Bethlehem 1889

The Arena of Song (with C.
C. Case) 1890

Florens, the Pilgrim 1890

The Wonderful Story . . . 1890

Jacob and Esau 1890

Christmas and Easter Selections annually from 1878
to 1890.

SHEET MUSIC.

Annie Lowe.
Away on the Prairie Alone.
Away! Away! the Track is White.
Battle-cry of Freedom.
Beautiful Maiden Just Over the Way.
Be Sure You Call as You Pass By.
Birds Have Sought the Forest Shade.
Bright-eyed Little Nell (Arranged).
Brother, Tell Me of the Battle.
Blow de Horn.
Can the Soldier Forget?
Columbia's Call.
Comrades, All Around is Brightness.
Come to Me Quickly.
Come, Oh! Come With Me.
Day of Columbia's Glory.
Dearest Spot of Earth to Me is Home.
Don't You See Me Coming?
Dreaming, Ever Dreaming.
Down the Line.
Dearest Brother, We Miss Thee.
Early Lost, Early Saved.
Eyes That are Watching.
Flying Home.
Father John.
Fare Thee Well! Kitty Dear.
Father Abraham's Reply.
Farewell! Father, Friend and Guardian.
First Gun is Fired.
Forward! Boys, Forward!
Fling Out the Flag!
Good Bye! Old Glory.
Glad to Get Home.

Gather up the Sunbeams.
God Bless Our Brave Young Volunteers!
Glory! Glory! Or the Little Octoroon.
Grieve not the Heart that Loves Thee.
Gently Wake the Song.
Greenwood Bell.
Hazel Dell.
Hasten on the Battle-field!
Hear, Hear, the Shout!
Hear the Cry that Comes Over the Sea!
Health is a Rosy Maiden.
He's Coming Again.
Home's Sweet Harmony.
Home Again Returning.
Honeysuckle Glen.
Have Ye Sharpened your Swords?
How it Marches, the Flag of Our Union!
Honor to Sheridan.
Homeless and Motherless.
He Giveth His Beloved Sleep.
Here in My Mountain Home.
Hunting Song.
Hundred Years Ago.
I'm Married.
I Ask No More.
Independent Farmer.
If He Can.
If Maggie Were My Own.
In the Storm.
I Dreamt an Angel Came.
I had a Gentle Mother.
Johnny, the Little Cripple's, Song.
Jenny Lyle.
Just before the Battle, Mother.

Just after the Battle.
Just over the Mountain.
Kind Friends, One and All.
Kiss Me, Mother, Kiss your Darling.
Kittie Ryan.
Liberty Bird.
Lay Me Down and Save the Flag!
Let Me Go!
Let Me Carry your Pail, Dear.
Laughing Song.
Love Thy Mother, Little One.
Love Lightens Labor.
Lo! The Clouds are Breaking.
Look on the Bright Side.
Mary of the Glen.
Mabel.
May Moore.
May of the Valley.
Music Far Away.
Mother, Sweet Mother, Why Linger Away.
Music of the Pine.
Mr. and Mrs. Williams.
My Cottage Home, Dear Mother.
My Mother, She is Sleeping.
My Beau that Went to Canada.
My Father's Bible.
My Heart is Like a Silent Lute.
My Weary Heart is All Alone.
No Section Lines.
North and South.
Never Forget the Dear Ones.
Nobody Cares.
New Voice in the Heavenly Choir.
O! Blow de Horn.
On, On, On, the Boys Came Marching.
On the Shore.

O! Are Ye Sleeping, Maggie? (Arranged.)
On Old Potomac's Shore.
Only Four.
Our Protective Union.
One Word.
Old Friends and True Friends.
On the Eve of Battle.
Only Waiting.
O! Will my Mother Never Come?
On! Boys, On!
O! Mother, Sing to Me of Heaven.
Pictures of Memory.
Poverty Flat.
Pity, O Savior! (Arranged.)
Poor Robin's Growing Old.
Poor Carlotta!
Rosalie, the Prairie Flower.
Reaper on the Plain.
Rock Me to Sleep, Mother.
Rosabel.
Rock, Rock the Cradle!
Sing, Birds and Brooks and Blossoms.
Sing Me to Sleep, Father.
See, the Sky is Darkling, Boys.
She has Told it to the Winds.
Softly, She Faded.
Somewhere.
So Long as Love is Left.
Scenes of Happiness, I Love Ye.
Starved in Prison.
Stand up for Uncle Sam, Boys!
Sweet Morn, How Lovely is thy Face!
Swinging All Day Long.
The Way is Long, My Darling.
They Have Broken up Their Camps.
The Liberty Bird.
The Mason's Home.

The Quiet Days When We Are Old.
The Road to Slumberland.
The Church Within the Wood.
The Father's Coming.
The Hidden Path.
The Forest Requiem.
The Hand that Holds the Bread.
The Miner's *Protegé*.
The New Voice In the Heavenly Choir.
The Price of a Drink.
The Star of Bethlehem.
The Old Canoe.
The Old Folks Are Gone.
Tramp! Tramp! Tramp!
The Trumpet Will Sound in the Morning.
The Time of the Heart.
There's Music in the Air.
They Sleep in the Dust.
That Little German Home. (Arranged.)
Touch the Keys Softly.

The Voice of Love.
The World as it is.
Turn the Other Way, Boys! (With J. R. Murray.)
Vacant Chair.
Voices of the Lake.
Wake! Lady, Wake!
We'll Fight it Out Here on the Old Union Line.
Within the Sound of the Enemy's Guns.
Who'll Save the Left?
What will People Say?
Where are the Wicked Folks Buried?
Where Earth and Heaven Meet.
When the Mail Comes in.
We are Going Away from the Old Home.
We can Make Home Happy.
We'll Meet in Heaven, Father.
Will you Come to Meet Me, Darling?
Yes, We'll be True to Each Other

My principal instrumental compositions are in the instruction books mentioned. Besides these there are two series in sheet form called respectively "Camps, Tramps, and Battle Fields" and "Home Scenes." There are besides—

The March of the 600,000
Italia Grand March.

WM. MASON.

Andante. Sempre e piano legato.

Slum - ber sweet-ly, dear-est, Close . . . thy

sweet - ly, Close thy

weary eyes, Guardian an-gels round thee hover Till the morning's

eyes, . . .

rise. Then may love on air-y pinions Bear thy heart in

trans-port bound To its own do-min-ions, Where no

earth-ly care is found. Maiden, sleep, sleep in peace.

A VOICE FROM THE LAKE.

Written for Geo. F. Root's Quartett
in 1847 by THEODOR EISFELD.

On the lake's unruf-fled sur - face Rests the moon's soft silv -'ry

beam ; Her pale wreath of roses wearing 'Mid the rush-es ver-dant

gleam, 'Mid the rush - es ver-dant gleam. Deer lie yon - der

near the mount-ain In the si - lent night a - wake,

Here and there the slen-der rushes Dreami-ly the birds will

shake, Dream-i - ly the birds will shake, While the

eyes are dim'd with weeping Deep within my soul I bear.

Thoughts of thee, sweet re-collection, Floating o'er me like a prayer,

Thoughts of thee

Thoughts of thee, sweet re-col-lec-tion Floating o'er me like a prayer,

Thoughts of thee, sweet recol - lection, Tho'ts of thee, sweet recollection,

Floating o'er me

Float - ing like a prayer, Floating o'er me like a prayer.

Float - ing like a

I WILL LAY ME DOWN IN PEACE.

I will both lay me down in peace and sleep, For thou, Lord, for

thou, Lord, on-ly makest me to dwell in safe - ty.

I will both lay me down in peace . . . pp

I will both lay me down in peace and sleep, and

I will both lay me down, will lay me down in peace

sleep, For thou, Lord, on-ly makest me to dwell in safe - ty.

G. F. Root.

There is a stream whose gen - tle flow Sup-

plies the cit - y of our God. Life,

love and joy.... still glid - ing through, And

wa - t'ring our...... di - vine ..... a - bode.

THE HAZEL DELL.

WURZEL.

In the Ha-zel Dell my Nelly's sleep-ing, Nel-ly loved so

long; And my lone-ly, lone-ly watch I'm keep - ing,

Nel-ly lost and gone; Here in moon-light oft - en we have

dar-ling Nel-ly's near me sleep - ing,— Nelly dear, fare-well.

dar-ling Nel-ly's near me sleep - ing,— Nelly dear, fare-well.

2. In the Ha - zel Dell my   Nel-ly's sleep-ing, Where the flow-ers
3. Now I'm wea-ry, friendless and for - sak - en, Watching here a-

wave, And the si - lent stars are nightly weep-ing O'er poor Nel-ly's
lone   Nelly, thou no more will fondly cheer me With thy lov - ing

grave; Hopes that once my bosom fondly cherished Smile no more on
tone; Yet for-ev - er shall thy gentle im - age In my mem-'ry

me; Ev'ry dream of joy, a-las, has perish'd, Nelly dear, with thee.
dwell; And my tears thy lonely grave shall moisten, Nelly dear, fare-well.

WURZEL. (G. F. R.)

Moderato.

1. On the dist - ant prai - rie, Where the heath-er wild
2. On that dist - ant prai - rie, When the days were long,
3. But the sum - mer fad - ed, And a chil - ly blast

In its qui - et beauty lived and smiled, Stands a lit - tle cottage,
Tripping like a fai - ry, sweet her song, With the sunny blos-soms
O'er that happy cot-tage swept at last, When the autumn song-birds

And a creep-ing vine Loves a - round its porch to
And the birds at play, Beau - ti - ful and bright as
Woke the dew - y morn, Lit - tle prai - rie flower was

twine;   In that peaceful dwelling was a love-ly child,
they;   When the twilight shadows gathered in the west,
gone;   For the an-gels whispered soft-ly in her ear,

With her blue eyes beaming soft and mild, And the wav-y ring-lets
And the voice of nature sunk to rest, Like a cherub kneeling
"Child, thy Father calls thee, stay not here," And they gently bore her,

of her flax-en hair, Waving in the sum-mer air.
seemed the lovely child, With her gentle eyes so mild.
robed in spotless white, To their blissful home of light.

CHORUS. (*Repeat pp*).

1 & 2. Fair as a li - ly, joyous and free, Light of that prairie home was she.

3. Tho' we shall never look on her more, Gone with the love and joy she bore,

Ev'ry one who knew her, felt the gentle pow'r of Rosalie the prairie flower.

Far away she's blooming in a fadeless bower, sweet Rosalie the prairie flower.

THE BATTLE CRY OF FREEDOM.

GEO. F. ROOT.

1. Yes, we'll ral-ly round the flag, boys, we'll ral-ly once a-gain,
2. We are springing to the call of our brothers gone be-fore,
3. We will wel-come to our numbers the loy-al, true and brave,
4. So we're springing to the call from the East and from the West,

Shouting the bat-tle cry of Freedom, We will ral-ly from the hill-
Shouting the bat-tle cry of Freedom, And we'll fill the vacant ranks
Shouting the bat-tle cry of Freedom, And al-tho' they may be poor,
Shouting the bat-tle cry of Freedom, And we'll hurl the reb-el crew

side, we'll gather from the plain, Shouting the battle cry of Freedom.
with a million freemen more, Shouting the battle cry of Freedom.
not a man shall be a slave, Shouting the battle cry of Freedom.
from the land we love the best, Shouting the battle cry of Freedom.

CHORUS. *ff*

The Un - ion for - ev - er, Hur-rah! boys, Hur-rah!

The Un - ion for - ev - er, Hur-rah! boys, Hur-rah!

Down with the trai - tor, Up with the star; While we

Down with the trai - tor, Up with the star; While we

ral - ly round the flag, boys, ral - ly once a - gain,

ral - ly round the flag, boys, ral - ly once a - gain,

Shout - ing the bat - tle cry of Free - dom.

Shout - ing the bat - tle cry of Free - dom.

GEO. F. ROOT.

Tenderly.

1. Just before the battle, Mother,   I am thinking most of you,
2. Oh, I long to see you, Mother, And the loving ones at home,
3. Hark! I hear the bugles sounding, 'Tis the signal for the fight,

While upon the field we're watching, With the en - e-my in view—
But I'll never leave our banner, Till in honor I can come
Now may God protect us, mother, As he ev-er does the right.

Comrades brave are round me ly-ing, Filled with tho'ts of home and God; For
Tell the traitors all around you, That their cruel words we know, In
Hear the "Battle-Cry of Freedom,"* How it swells upon the air, Oh,

* In some of the divisions of our army the "Battle-Cry" is sung, when going into action, by order of the commanding officers.

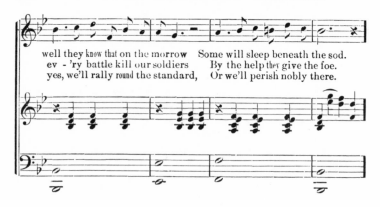

well they know that on the morrow   Some will sleep beneath the sod.
ev - 'ry battle kill our soldiers   By the help they give the foe.
yes, we'll rally round the standard,   Or we'll perish nobly there.

CHORUS.

Fare - well, Mother, you may nev - er

you may nev - er, Mother,

Fare - well, Mother, you may nev - er, you may nev - er, Mother,

Press me to your heart a - gain; But oh, you'll not forget me,

Press me to your heart a - gain; But oh, you'll not forget me,

Rit. **Repeat** *pp*

Mother, If I'm numbere'd with the slain.

you will not forget me,

Mother, you will not forget me, If I'm numbere'd with the slain.

TRAMP! TRAMP! TRAMP!

GEO. F. ROOT.

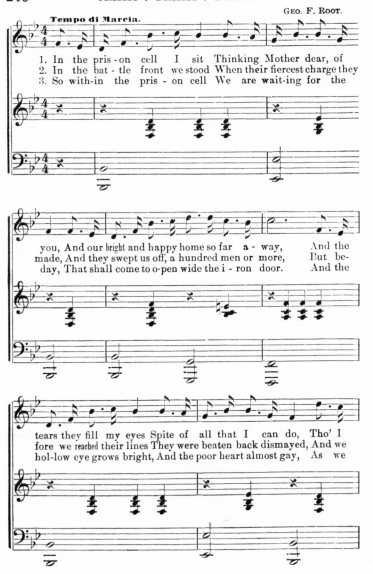

Tempo di Marcia.

1. In the pris-on cell I sit Thinking Mother dear, of
2. In the bat-tle front we stood When their fiercest charge they
3. So with-in the pris-on cell We are wait-ing for the

you, And our bright and happy home so far a - way, And the
made, And they swept us off, a hundred men or more, But be-
day, That shall come to o-pen wide the i - ron door. And the

tears they fill my eyes Spite of all that I can do, Tho' I
fore we reached their lines They were beaten back dismayed, And we
hol-low eye grows bright, And the poor heart almost gay, As we

try   to cheer my com-rades and be   gay.
heard the cry   of vic - t'ry o'er and o'er.
think of   see - ing home and friends once more.

When the chorus is sung, this may be omitted after the first verse.

Tramp, tramp, tramp, the boys are march-ing, Cheer up, comrades,
Tramp, tramp, tramp, the boys are march-ing, Cheer up, comrades,
Tramp, tramp, tramp, the boys are march-ing, Cheer up, comrades,

they will come,   And be-neath the star - ry flag We shall
they will come,   And be-neath the star - ry flag We shall
they will come,   And be-neath the star - ry flag We shall

When the chorus is not sung, end here.

breathe the air a-gain, Of the free-land in our own beloved home.
breathe the air a-gain, Of the free-land in our own beloved home.
breathe the air a-gain, Of the free-land in our own beloved home.

CHORUS.

Tramp, tramp, tramp, the boys are march - ing, Cheer up, comrades,

marching on, O cheer up, com -

Tramp, tramp, tramp, the boys are march-ing on, O cheer up, com -

they will come,   And beneath the star-ry flag We shall

rades,   they   will   come,

rades,   they   will   come, And beneath the star-ry flag We shall

breathe the air   a-gain, Of the free-land in our own beloved   home.

breathe the air   a-gain, Of the free-land in our own beloved   home.

THE VACANT CHAIR.

N. S. W.

GEO. F. ROOT.

With expression.

1. We shall meet, but we shall miss him, There will be   one vacant
2. At our fire - side, sad and lonely,   Often will   the bo-som
3. True they tell   us wreaths of glo-ry   Ev-er more will deck his

chair;   We shall lin - ger to ca - ress him   While we
swell,   At re-mem - brance of the sto - ry   How our
brow,   But this soothes the an-guish on - ly   Sweeping

breathe   our even-ing prayer.   When a year   a - go we
no - ble   Wil-lie   fell;   How he strove to bear our
o'er   our heart-strings now.   Sleep to-day,   oh, ear - ly

gathered, Joy was in his mild blue eye, But a
ban-ner Thro' the thick - est of the fight, And up-
fall-en, In thy green and nar-row bed, Dirg-es

gold-en chord is severed, And our hopes in ru-in lie.
hold our country's honor, In the strength of manhood's might.
from the pine and cypress Mingle with the tears we shed.

CHORUS.

We shall meet, but we shall miss him, There will be one vacant

We shall meet, but we shall miss him, There will be one vacant

chair; We shall lin-ger to caress him, When we breathe our evening

chair; We shall lin-ger to caress him, When we breathe our evening

prayer.

prayer.

FOR MENS' VOICES.*   G. F. ROOT.

1. There's music in the air, When the infant morn is nigh, And
2. There's music in the air, When the noontide's sul-t'ry beam Re-
3. There's music in the air, When the twilight's gen-tle sigh Is

faint its blush is seen On the bright and laughing sky.
flects a gold-en light On the distant mount-ain stream.
lost on evening's breast, As its pensive beauties die.

* If sung by mixed voices, let the alto be an octave lower.

Many a harp's ec - stat - ic sound   With its thrill of

When beneath some grateful shade   Sorrow's ach-ing

Then, O then the loved ones gone   Wake the pure ce-

joy pro-found,   While we list en - chant-ed there   To the

head is laid,   Sweetly to the spi - rit there Comes the

les - tial song,   An-gel voic - es greet us there   In the

mu - sic in the air.

mu - sic in the air.

mu - sic in the air.

THE SHINING SHORE.

Rev. DAVID NELSON. G. F. ROOT.

1. My days are glid-ing swift-ly by, And I, a pilgrim stranger,
2. We'll gird our loins, my brethren dear, Our heav'nly home discerning;

Would not de-tain them as they fly, Those hours of toil and danger.
Our ab-sent Lord has left us word, Let ev-'ry lamp be burn-ing.

CHORUS.

For oh, we stand on Jordan's strand, Our friends are passing o - ver;

And just be - fore the Shining Shore We may almost discov - er.

3 Should coming days be cold and dark,
   We need not cease our singing;
   That perfect rest naught can molest,
   Where golden harps are ringing.

4 Let sorrow's rudest tempests blow,
   Each chord on earth to sever;
   Our King says, Come, and there's our home,
   Forever, oh, forever.